"Hire character. Train skill"

– Peter Schutz

PREFACE

The landscape of work is experiencing a profound transformation, driven by rapid technological advancements, evolving generational expectations, and the widespread adoption of virtual and hybrid work models. These shifts are reshaping the way organizations function, and at the heart of this change lies the critical synergy between Human Resources (HR) and Organizational Behavior (OB). In today's dynamic work environment, both disciplines are indispensable to the growth and sustainability of modern workplaces.

This book is crafted as a comprehensive guide for professionals, students, and leaders striving to navigate and thrive in this new world of work. It delves deeply into the challenges and opportunities HR and OB face in contemporary organizations, offering insights, strategies, and practical solutions to address them effectively.

The journey begins by exploring the foundational concepts of HR and OB in the modern workplace, with a special focus on the importance of people-centric management. As organizations recognize that their employees are their greatest asset, this shift towards prioritizing human capital becomes central to achieving success in the 21st century. From this foundation, the book progresses to the complexities and nuances of virtual and hybrid organizations, providing guidance on how businesses can adapt and excel in these evolving work models.

As the workforce undergoes a demographic shift with Millennials and Gen Z coming into their own, recruitment and talent acquisition strategies must evolve. We examine the cutting-edge tools and techniques shaping hiring practices today, from Artificial Intelligence (AI) and Machine Learning (ML) to the revolutionary potential of blockchain in HR. Automation, while a powerful ally, brings its own set of challenges. We explore how organizations can harness its capabilities without losing sight of human touch, ensuring a seamless integration of technology and people.

An extra critical area covered is performance management, where the adoption of Objectives and Key Results (OKRs) and Key Performance Indicators (KPIs) plays a pivotal role in aligning individual goals with organizational success. As a consequence, as businesses strive to stay competitive, upskilling and reskilling the workforce are not just trends, but imperatives. Pay transparency and equity are also key pillars discussed, as organizations that foster a culture of fairness and openness are better positioned to engage and retain top talent.

Employee retention, one of the most pressing issues in HR today, is addressed with actionable strategies that emphasize the significance of emotional intelligence, self-awareness, and high-performing teams. The creation of inclusive cultures, along with the ability to measure the success of Diversity, Equity, and Inclusion (DEI) initiatives, is a crucial focus area. We also delve into sustainability practices and the rise of employee advocacy, understanding their role in shaping both corporate identity and employee engagement.

The gig economy and remote work have redefined traditional employment models. We analyze how these trends are impacting HR and OB practices, offering fresh perspectives on how organizations can support a flexible, diverse, and remote workforce. Too, we explore the psychological aspects of organizational change, focusing on the Change Curve and the adaptability of employees in an ever-shifting workplace. Mental health initiatives, now more critical than ever, are explored in detail, reflecting their significance in fostering a supportive, inclusive, and productive work culture.

For students and aspiring HR professionals, this book provides actionable insights on applying OB principles to real-world scenarios, as well as guidance on how to build a thriving career in HR. The evolving role of HR and OB professionals is also examined, highlighting their strategic importance in shaping the future of work.

This book is the result of extensive research, expert insights, and practical strategies designed to equip readers with the tools they need to succeed in the modern workplace. Whether you are a student, a practicing HR professional, or a business leader, our hope is that this work inspires you to embrace the challenges and opportunities of this new era, fostering workplaces that are inclusive, innovative, and human-centric.

Welcome to the future of work. Together, let's redefine it.

— Dr. Dhanashree Chaudhari & Dr. Deepali Patil

BOOK INDEX

INTRODUCTION

The transition from academia to the corporate world is one of the most defining phases of a professional's life. College classrooms equip students with theoretical knowledge, but the workplace demands a blend of skills, adaptability, and a deep understanding of human behavior in organizations. *Campus to Corporate* is a comprehensive guide designed to help students, young professionals, and HR practitioners navigate the complexities of modern workplaces.

With the rise of technology, remote work, and evolving workforce expectations, organizations are redefining how they function. Employees today are no longer just resources— they are the heart of an enterprise. The modern workplace thrives on people-centric management, data-driven decision-making, and a human-first approach. This book unpacks the critical aspects of HR and Organizational Behavior (OB) that every aspiring professional needs to master.

The corporate world today is vastly different from what it was a decade ago. The shift towards virtual and hybrid organizations has redefined how teams collaborate and function. Companies are leveraging cutting-edge technology, including AI (Artificial Intelligence), ML (Machine Learning), and Blockchain, to streamline HR processes, from recruitment to performance management. Nonetheless, while automation is reshaping HR, the human touch remains irreplaceable.

This book explores how AI is transforming hiring by making recruitment more efficient while also addressing concerns about bias and ethical AI use. Millennials and Gen Z, who are becoming dominant in the workforce, have different expectations regarding job roles, workplace culture, and career growth. Recruitment strategies need to evolve to attract and retain this talent pool effectively.

The corporate landscape is continuously evolving with the rise of the gig economy and remote work. Employees today seek flexibility and work-life balance, prompting businesses to rethink their policies. Meanwhile, sustainability has become a crucial factor, with organizations encouraging employee advocacy for environmental and social causes.

Change is inevitable, and professionals must adapt to organizational transformations effectively. The Change Curve model helps employees understand their reactions to change and how to navigate through transitions successfully. As a consequence, mental health in the workplace has gained significant attention, and companies are now investing in initiatives to support employees' psychological well-being.

For students stepping into the corporate world, understanding Organizational Behavior (OB) can be a game-changer. OB principles help individuals manage workplace dynamics, resolve conflicts, and contribute to a positive work culture. This book provides practical insights into how students can apply OB theories in their day-to-day professional lives.

At that, for those interested in a career in HR, this book outlines the essential skills and strategies required to succeed in this domain. With HR roles evolving rapidly, professionals must stay ahead by embracing technology, data-driven decision-making, and human-centric leadership.

Campus to Corporate is more than just a guide—it is a roadmap to a fulfilling and successful career. Whether you are stepping into the corporate world or looking to refine your HR strategies, this book will equip you with the knowledge, tools, and insights to thrive in the modern workplace.

Are you ready to embrace the future of work?

Let's begin...

Have a happy reading!

1. DEFINING HR AND OB IN MODERN WORKPLACES

The modern workplace is a dynamic, ever-evolving ecosystem shaped by technological advancements, cultural shifts, and changing employee expectations. At the core of this transformation lies the interplay between Human Resources (HR) and Organizational Behavior (OB), two disciplines that have become indispensable in navigating the complexities of today's work environments. This chapter aims to define HR and OB in the context of modern workplaces, particularly within the Indian organizational landscape, and explore their evolving roles in driving organizational success.

Author's Creation

Human Resources (HR): Beyond Administrative Functions

Human Resources (HR) refers to the strategic management of an organization's most valuable asset—its people. It involves recruiting, developing, and retaining talent while creating policies and programs to ensure employees are aligned with organizational goals and engaged in their work. HR's key functions include workforce planning, compensation and benefits, training and development, performance management, and ensuring legal and ethical compliance. In modern organizations, HR is not just about administrative functions; it plays a strategic role in shaping organizational culture, improving employee experience, and driving overall business success.

Author: Dessler, G. (2020). Human Resource Management (15th ed.). Pearson.

Normally, HR was perceived as a support function primarily responsible for administrative tasks such as payroll processing, recruitment, and compliance. Still, the role of HR has undergone a significant transformation in recent years. In modern workplaces, HR is no longer just a back-office function but a strategic partner that contributes to organizational growth, employee engagement, and cultural development.

In India, the shift in HR's role is evident in the way organizations are prioritizing employee experience and well-being. A 2022 study by Deloitte India highlighted that 78% of Indian organizations are investing in HR technologies to enhance employee engagement and streamline processes. From talent acquisition to performance management, HR professionals are now leveraging data analytics, artificial intelligence (AI), and machine learning (ML) to make informed decisions. For instance, companies like Infosys and

Tata Consultancy Services (TCS) have adopted AI-driven tools for recruitment and employee development, reflecting the growing emphasis on innovation in HR practices.

Conjointly the COVID-19 pandemic accelerated the adoption of remote and hybrid work models, pushing HR teams to rethink their strategies. According to a 2023 report by McKinsey, 65% of Indian organizations have implemented flexible work policies, with HR playing a pivotal role in ensuring seamless transitions and maintaining employee morale. This shift underscores the strategic importance of HR in fostering adaptability and resilience in the face of change.

Organizational Behavior (OB): Understanding Human Dynamics

Organizational Behavior (OB) is the study of how individuals and groups behave within an organization and how this behavior impacts organizational performance. OB explores various factors that influence behavior in the workplace, such as motivation, leadership, team dynamics, communication, and organizational culture. By understanding these behaviors, OB aims to improve organizational effectiveness, enhance employee satisfaction, and foster positive work environments. OB integrates insights from psychology, sociology, and management theories to address workplace challenges and optimize organizational functioning.

Author: Robbins, S. P., & Judge, T. A. (2019). Organizational Behavior (18th ed.). Pearson.

Organizational Behavior (OB) is the study of how individuals and groups interact within an organization and how these interactions influence organizational performance. It encompasses a wide range of topics, including motivation, leadership, communication, and team dynamics. In modern workplaces, OB provides valuable insights into human behavior, helping organizations create environments that promote productivity, collaboration, and innovation.

In the Indian context, OB has gained prominence as organizations strive to build inclusive and high-performing cultures. A 2023 study by the Indian School of Business (ISB) revealed that companies with strong OB practices reported a 20% increase in employee satisfaction and a 15% improvement in productivity. For example, Hindustan Unilever (HUL) has been recognized for its focus on leadership development and employee empowerment, which are rooted in OB principles. By fostering a culture of trust and transparency, HUL has been able to attract and retain top talent, setting a benchmark for other Indian organizations.

The rise of remote work has also brought OB to the forefront, as managers grapple with challenges such as virtual team dynamics and employee engagement. A recent survey by NASSCOM found that 60% of Indian employees prefer hybrid work models, highlighting the need for OB-driven strategies to address the unique challenges of dispersed teams. Organizations are increasingly investing in training programs to enhance emotional intelligence, communication skills, and conflict resolution capabilities among leaders, reflecting the growing recognition of OB's role in driving organizational success.

The Synergy Between HR and OB

While HR and OB are distinct disciplines, their synergy is critical in modern workplaces. HR provides the structural framework for managing people, while OB offers the psychological and behavioral insights needed to optimize human potential. Together, they enable organizations to create workplaces that are not only efficient but also humane and inclusive.

In India, this synergy is evident in the way organizations are addressing diversity, equity, and inclusion (DEI). A 2023 report by LinkedIn revealed that 70% of Indian companies have implemented DEI initiatives, with HR and OB working hand in hand to foster inclusive cultures. For instance, Wipro has launched several programs aimed at promoting gender diversity and mental well-being, reflecting the integration of HR practices and OB principles.

Challenges Faced by Indian Organizations

Technological Transformation The rapid pace of technological change is both a challenge and an opportunity for Indian organizations. While larger urban-based companies are quick to adopt new technologies such as Artificial Intelligence, automation, and cloud computing, many smaller businesses in rural and semi-urban regions continue to struggle with the resources required to make these technological upgrades. This creates a digital divide within the organizational landscape, making it difficult for businesses to maintain uniformity in HR and OB practices across regions.

Diverse Workforce and Cultural Differences India's vast and diverse cultural fabric poses another challenge for HR and

OB professionals. Organizations in India often need to tailor their human resource strategies to cater to a wide array of cultural values, regional practices, and language barriers. In a country where traditional mindsets sometimes dominate, the adoption of modern HR practices can face resistance. Employees in rural areas, for example, may find it difficult to adjust to corporate cultures that are more prevalent in urban areas. This gap can affect overall employee engagement and retention.

Resource Constraints in Smaller Enterprises In India, especially in the small and medium-sized enterprises (SMEs) sector, there are often limited resources for HR and OB initiatives. Many SMEs do not have dedicated HR departments or the capacity to implement modern organizational behavior practices, such as employee well-being programs or leadership development initiatives. Consequently, these organizations may miss out on the benefits of structured HR management, which can hinder their growth and sustainability.

Opportunities for Innovation

While these challenges are significant, they also open up several opportunities for innovation and growth within Indian organizations.

Sustainability and Corporate Social Responsibility (CSR) A growing focus on sustainability and CSR in India is transforming how companies approach HR and OB. Leading organizations like ITC and Mahindra & Mahindra have effectively integrated sustainability into their HR strategies. These companies align their employees' personal goals with broader organizational objectives, focusing on creating value not just for shareholders, but also for the community and environment. By incorporating sustainability into HR practices, Indian organizations can foster a sense of purpose among employees, which, in turn, can enhance engagement, loyalty, and overall job satisfaction.

Strategic Role of HR and OB The role of HR and OB has evolved dramatically over the years. Today, they are not just administrative functions, but strategic pillars within the organization. In the Indian context, HR and OB have shifted from merely managing personnel to being involved in shaping organizational culture, improving employee productivity, and driving business outcomes. This transformation is particularly important for industries undergoing digital and global transformations, where skilled human capital is the key to success.

Employee Expectations and Work-Life Balance As globalization influences the Indian workforce, employees are becoming increasingly aware of the global standards for work-life balance, career development, and job satisfaction. They now expect their employers to focus on their overall well-being, including mental health support, flexible working hours, and a culture of inclusivity. Indian organizations can seize this opportunity by redesigning HR policies to meet these growing demands. By adopting a more people-centric approach, organizations can boost employee morale, engagement, and retention, while simultaneously enhancing productivity.

The Future of HR and OB in India

As we look ahead, the integration of HR and OB practices will become even more crucial in addressing the future challenges Indian organizations face. The post-pandemic world has ushered in the era of remote and hybrid work, making it essential for HR professionals to manage teams that may be geographically dispersed. This shift requires a new approach to communication, collaboration, and performance management. Further, with the growing awareness of mental health issues, HR professionals must play an active role in promoting well-being and providing resources for employees to cope with stress, anxiety, and burnout.

For HR and OB professionals, the future lies in continuous learning, adaptability, and embracing innovative approaches to employee engagement and organizational development. To build resilient and high-performing workplaces, HR must not only focus on attracting talent but also on nurturing and retaining it through personalized experiences that cater to the diverse needs of employees.

As author mentioned earlier, the journey to redefine HR and OB in Indian organizations is ongoing. While challenges persist, they present significant opportunities to create more sustainable, inclusive, and innovative workplaces. HR and OB professionals, in collaboration with organizational leaders, must continue to drive this change, ensuring that organizations are better equipped to thrive in an ever-evolving business environment.

2. THE IMPORTANCE OF PEOPLE-CENTRIC MANAGEMENT IN MODERN WORKPLACES

People-Centric Management is a leadership approach that prioritizes the needs, development, and well-being of employees while aligning them with the organization's goals and values. This management style recognizes employees as the most valuable asset of the organization and focuses on creating an environment where they are empowered, motivated, and supported. A people-centric approach involves providing opportunities for growth, fostering a positive organizational culture, and ensuring work-life balance, as well as valuing employee feedback and engagement. It encourages organizations to shift from traditional top-down management to a more inclusive, participative, and collaborative model.

Author: Ulrich, D., & Dulebohn, J. H. (2015). Are we there yet? What we know about the future of HR and organizational behavior. Human Resource Management Review, 25(3), 264-275.

In the ever-evolving landscape of modern workplaces, the concept of people-centric management has emerged as a cornerstone of organizational success. Unlike traditional management approaches that prioritize processes and profits, people-centric management places employees at the heart of decision-making, recognizing that their well-being, engagement, and growth are integral to achieving sustainable business outcomes. This chapter explores the significance of people-centric management, particularly in the context of Indian organizations, and highlights its transformative impact on workplace culture, productivity, and innovation.

The Shift Toward People-Centric Management in Indian Organizations

The business landscape across the globe has been undergoing a significant transformation in recent years, particularly in terms of how organizations view and manage their workforce. With technological advancements, changes in workforce demographics, and the rise of the knowledge economy, organizations are increasingly recognizing that their employees are not just resources but valuable assets who contribute directly to organizational success. This shift is particularly evident in India, where the workforce is young, dynamic, and highly adaptable, presenting both opportunities and challenges for businesses.

The Changing Role of Employees

In the past, employees were often seen as mere cogs in the organizational machine, expected to perform specific tasks and deliver results. While, this traditional view is rapidly changing. Today, employees are seen as key drivers of success, whose potential, creativity, and innovation can propel an organization forward. The emergence of a knowledge-based economy in India, where the value of information, creativity, and expertise is high, has made this shift even more critical. In this environment, companies can no longer afford to treat employees as expendable resources but must focus on building a culture where employees feel valued and empowered.

The Rise of People-Centric Management

In India, a country known for its large and diverse workforce, the emphasis on people-centric management practices has become more pronounced. Management professionals and HR leaders are recognizing that creating a positive workplace culture and adopting employee-friendly policies are no longer just "nice to have" initiatives—they are essential for attracting, engaging, and retaining top talent. This is particularly important in the current scenario, where the younger generation of employees is more inclined to work for organizations that prioritize their well-being and growth.

A 2023 report by the Boston Consulting Group (BCG) highlighted that 85% of Indian employees consider workplace culture and employee-centric policies as crucial factors in their job satisfaction. This statistic sheds light on the growing importance of people-centric practices in Indian organizations, where employees want to feel valued not only for their skills but also for their overall well-being.

Leading Indian Companies Driving the Change

Several prominent Indian organizations have recognized the need for a people-centric approach and are leading the way with innovative practices.

Tata Steel: Tata Steel, one of India's oldest and most respected companies, has long been known for its focus on employee welfare. The company places a high priority on creating a supportive and inclusive workplace culture. Tata Steel has implemented numerous initiatives to enhance employee engagement, career growth, and overall well-being. This includes comprehensive health and wellness programs, career development plans, and family support initiatives. The company has also been instrumental in creating leadership programs that nurture future leaders within the organization.

HDFC Bank: HDFC Bank, one of India's leading private-sector banks, has also made significant strides toward people-centric management. The bank has focused on employee satisfaction by offering flexible working conditions, opportunities for skill development, and competitive compensation packages. In remarking point, HDFC Bank has introduced work-life balance programs, such as wellness and fitness initiatives, which are aimed at reducing employee stress and improving mental health. These efforts not only help in enhancing employee morale but also boost productivity and loyalty.

Key Principles of People-Centric Management

People-centric management is built on several key principles that differentiate it from traditional management approaches:

1. **Employee Well-Being:** At the core of people-centric management is the belief that employees' physical, mental, and emotional well-being directly impacts their performance. Indian organizations are increasingly investing in wellness programs, mental health initiatives, and flexible work arrangements to support their employees. For instance, Infosys has introduced comprehensive mental health programs, including counselling services and stress management workshops, to address the growing prevalence of workplace stress.

2. **Empowerment and Autonomy:** People-centric management emphasizes empowering employees by giving them the autonomy to make decisions and take ownership of their work. This approach fosters a sense of accountability and encourages innovation. A study by the Indian Institute of Management (IIM) Ahmedabad found that organizations that promote employee autonomy report higher levels of creativity and job satisfaction. Companies like Flipkart and Zomato have embraced this principle by creating flat organizational structures and encouraging cross-functional collaboration.

3. **Continuous Learning and Development:** In a rapidly changing business environment, continuous learning is essential for both employees and organizations. People-centric management prioritizes upskilling and reskilling initiatives to help employees stay relevant and competitive. According to a 2023 survey by LinkedIn, 72% of Indian organizations have increased their investment in learning and development programs over the past two years. Wipro's "TopGear" initiative, which focuses on

upskilling employees in emerging technologies, is a prime example of this trend.

4. **Inclusive and Diverse Workplaces:** People-centric management recognizes the value of diversity and inclusion in driving innovation and fostering a sense of belonging. Indian organizations are increasingly adopting policies to promote gender diversity, support underrepresented groups, and create inclusive cultures. A 2023 report by Deloitte India highlighted that companies with diverse leadership teams are 1.7 times more likely to be innovation leaders in their industries.

The Impact of People-Centric Management

The adoption of people-centric management practices has far-reaching implications for organizations, employees, and society at large. Research has consistently shown that organizations that prioritize their people outperform their peers in terms of productivity, employee retention, and financial performance.

Enhanced Employee Engagement: People-centric management fosters a sense of purpose and belonging among employees, leading to higher levels of engagement. A 2023 study by Gallup found that organizations with high employee engagement report 21% higher productivity and 22% higher profitability. In India, companies like Godrej and Mahindra & Mahindra have achieved remarkable success by creating employee-centric cultures that emphasize recognition, feedback, and open communication.

Improved Retention and Talent Attraction: In a competitive job market, people-centric management can be a key differentiator for attracting and retaining top talent. A 2023 survey by NASSCOM revealed that 68% of Indian employees are more likely to stay with an employer that prioritizes their well-being and professional growth. Tech giants like TCS and Wipro have leveraged their people-centric policies to build strong employer brands and reduce attrition rates.

Driving Innovation and Agility: By empowering employees and fostering a culture of collaboration, people-centric management enables organizations to adapt to change and drive innovation. A 2023 report by McKinsey highlighted that Indian companies with people-centric cultures are 1.5 times more likely to be agile and innovative. Startups like Byju's and Ola have demonstrated this by encouraging experimentation and rewarding creative problem-solving.

Challenges in Implementing People-Centric Management

While the benefits of people-centric management are undeniable, its implementation is not without challenges. In India, organizations often face barriers such as resistance to change, lack of leadership buy-in, and resource constraints. That is why, the diverse cultural and socio-economic landscape of the country requires tailored approaches to address the unique needs of different employee groups.

Even so, these challenges also present opportunities for innovation. For example, the rise of digital tools and platforms has made it easier for organizations to implement people-centric practices at scale. Companies like Reliance Industries and HCL Technologies have leveraged technology to enhance employee engagement, streamline communication, and provide personalized learning experiences.

People-centric management is no longer a luxury but a necessity in modern workplaces. In the Indian context, its importance is amplified by the country's young, aspirational workforce and the rapid pace of economic and technological change. By prioritizing employee well-being, empowerment, and growth, organizations can unlock the full potential of their people and achieve sustainable success.

As we move forward, the adoption of people-centric management practices will be critical in addressing the challenges of the future, from managing remote teams to fostering diversity and inclusion. The journey toward becoming a people-centric organization is ongoing, and its success will depend on the collective efforts of leaders, managers, and employees alike.

3. VIRTUAL AND HYBRID ORGANIZATIONS: REDEFINING THE FUTURE OF WORK IN INDIA

The COVID-19 pandemic served as a catalyst for one of the most significant shifts in the world of work: the rise of virtual and hybrid organizations. What began as a temporary response to lockdowns and social distancing measures has now evolved into a permanent transformation, reshaping how organizations operate and how employees experience work. In India, a country known for its diverse workforce and rapidly growing economy, the adoption of virtual and hybrid work models has been both a challenge and an opportunity. This chapter explores the emergence of virtual and hybrid organizations in India, their impact on workplace dynamics, and the strategies needed to thrive in this new era.

The Rise of Virtual and Hybrid Work Models in Indian Organizations

The global business environment has undergone a profound shift, with organizations embracing new work models to adapt to changing dynamics. This transformation has been particularly evident in India, where virtual and hybrid work models have gained significant traction. Virtual organizations, which operate entirely online, enable employees to work remotely and collaborate using digital tools. In contrast, hybrid organizations combine both remote work and in-office presence, offering employees the flexibility to choose where and how they work. This shift has been fueled by several factors, including advancements in technology, changing employee preferences, and the need for business continuity, especially during the COVID-19 pandemic.

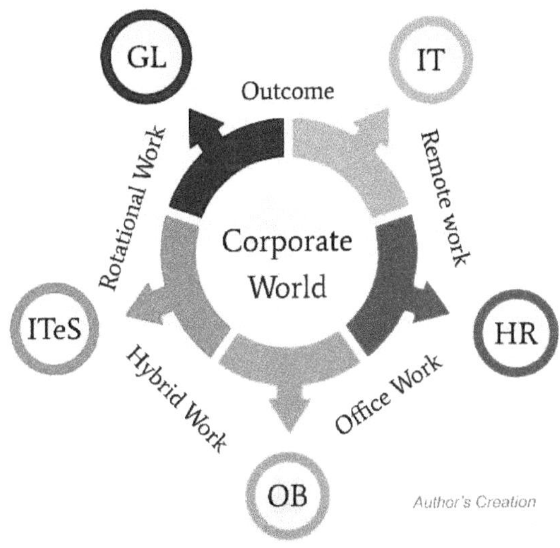

The pandemic acted as a catalyst for this change, forcing organizations to rethink how work could be performed in a more flexible and decentralized manner. As businesses navigated the uncertainties brought on by the pandemic, many realized the benefits of having a workforce that was not bound by geographical constraints. Technology played a key role in enabling remote work, allowing employees to stay connected and productive from home or other remote locations. With tools such as video conferencing, collaboration platforms, and cloud storage, organizations were able to maintain continuity and efficiency, even when physical offices were closed.

In India, a country known for its diverse workforce and fast-evolving business environment, the shift to virtual and hybrid work models has been particularly pronounced in industries such as Information Technology (IT) and IT-enabled services (ITeS). Companies in these sectors were already well-positioned to embrace digital solutions and had the infrastructure in place to support remote work. For instance, leading organizations like Tata Consultancy Services (TCS), Infosys, and Wipro were quick to implement flexible work-from-anywhere policies. These companies not only responded to the immediate challenges of the pandemic but also began to see the long-term advantages of offering employees the freedom to work remotely.

TCS, for example, introduced its "25/25" vision, which aims to have only 25% of its workforce in offices at any given time by 2025. This ambitious initiative reflects a broader trend within the Indian corporate landscape towards decentralization and flexibility. By reducing the need for employees to be physically present in offices, organizations can create a more agile and responsive workforce, one that can adapt quickly to changing market conditions and customer needs. Too, it allows companies to tap into a broader talent pool, not just in urban centers but also in smaller towns and rural areas, where employees can now contribute to the organization without the need to relocate.

The hybrid work model, which combines both remote and in-office work, has proven to be particularly appealing to many employees in India. The flexibility it offers allows individuals to balance their personal and professional lives more effectively. For example, employees can work from home when they need to focus on deep work or manage family responsibilities, while still being able to come into the office for collaboration and team-building activities. This model has been particularly important in India, where long commute times in major cities can be a significant source of stress and inefficiency for employees. By offering the option to work remotely, organizations can reduce commuting time, improve employee satisfaction, and increase overall productivity.

A 2023 report by NASSCOM revealed that 65% of Indian organizations have adopted hybrid work models, and 25% have transitioned to fully virtual operations. These statistics highlight a significant shift in the Indian corporate landscape, with organizations increasingly recognizing the importance of offering flexible work arrangements. While hybrid models have gained widespread popularity across industries, fully virtual operations are still more common in the IT and ITeS sectors, where digital tools and remote collaboration have become integral to daily operations.

The rise of virtual and hybrid work models in India is not just about responding to the immediate challenges posed by the pandemic but is also a reflection of broader changes in employee expectations. Today's workforce, particularly among younger generations, is more focused on work-life balance, flexibility, and the ability to work remotely. This shift in employee preferences has forced organizations to rethink their approach to work and embrace new models that prioritize employee well-being and autonomy. As a result, many Indian organizations are investing in technology and infrastructure to support remote work, ensuring that employees have the tools they need to collaborate effectively and remain engaged.

Anyway the transition to virtual and hybrid work models also presents challenges. Managing remote teams requires new leadership strategies and communication practices. Managers must focus more on outcomes and results rather than micromanaging daily tasks, which can be difficult in a culture that has consistently emphasized close supervision. Over and above, organizations must find ways to maintain a strong sense of team cohesion and company culture in a virtual or hybrid environment, where face-to-face interactions are limited.

Regardless these challenges, the shift toward virtual and hybrid work models present several opportunities for organizations in India. One of the key advantages is the ability to attract and retain talent from a wider geographic area. With the flexibility to work remotely, organizations can tap into talent pools outside of major metropolitan areas, where the competition for skilled professionals is often intense. This can be particularly valuable in a country like India, where the workforce is large and diverse, and talent is often concentrated in a few urban hubs.

As a consequence, the cost savings associated with virtual and hybrid work models can be significant. By reducing the need for large office spaces, companies can lower their overhead costs. This is especially relevant in India's high-cost urban centers, where real estate prices are rising rapidly. With fewer employees in the office at any given time, organizations can reduce their real estate footprint and invest the savings into other areas, such as employee development, technology, and innovation.

The hybrid and virtual work models also offer opportunities for organizations to foster greater inclusivity and diversity. By removing geographical constraints, companies can hire talent from diverse backgrounds, regions, and communities, creating a more inclusive work environment. Erog, remote work can be a game-changer for employees with disabilities or those who require flexible working hours due to family or personal commitments.

As India continues to experience rapid economic growth and technological advancement, the rise of virtual and hybrid work models is likely to shape the future of work in the country. For management students, HR professionals, and OB experts, understanding the dynamics of these work models is essential. The ability to effectively manage remote and hybrid teams, foster employee engagement in a virtual environment, and leverage technology to drive collaboration will be crucial skills for future leaders. By embracing these new work models, organizations in India can build more agile, inclusive, and resilient workplaces, positioning themselves for long-term success in an increasingly digital and interconnected world.

Challenges of Virtual and Hybrid Organizations

For all their benefits, virtual and hybrid work models present unique challenges that Indian organizations must address:

Digital Divide and Infrastructure Gaps: While urban employees have access to high-speed internet and advanced technology, those in rural and semi-urban areas often face connectivity issues and inadequate infrastructure. A 2023 study by the Indian Council for Research on International Economic Relations (ICRIER) found that 40% of remote workers in India struggle with unreliable internet access, hindering their productivity.

Maintaining Collaboration and Culture: Virtual and hybrid work can lead to feelings of isolation and disconnection among employees. Building a cohesive organizational culture and fostering collaboration in a dispersed workforce require intentional efforts. Companies like HCL Technologies have addressed this challenge by organizing virtual team-building activities and using collaboration tools like Microsoft Teams and Slack.

Performance Monitoring and Accountability: Ensuring accountability and measuring performance in remote settings can be challenging for managers. A 2023 survey by KPMG India revealed that 55% of Indian managers find it difficult to evaluate employee performance in virtual and hybrid environments. To address this, organizations are adopting outcome-based performance metrics and leveraging AI-driven analytics tools.

Data Security and Privacy: The shift to remote work has increased the risk of data breaches and cyberattacks. A 2023 report by PwC India highlighted that 60% of Indian organizations experienced a rise in cybersecurity incidents during the pandemic. To mitigate these risks, companies are investing in robust cybersecurity measures and employee training programs.

Strategies for Success in Virtual and Hybrid Organizations

To thrive in the era of virtual and hybrid work, Indian organizations must adopt a strategic and holistic approach:

1. **Investing in Technology and Infrastructure:** Providing employees with the tools and resources they need to work effectively is critical. This includes high-speed internet, collaboration platforms, and cybersecurity solutions. For example, Reliance Jio has partnered with several organizations to offer affordable internet packages for remote workers.

2. **Reimagining Workplace Policies:** Organizations must update their policies to reflect the realities of virtual and hybrid work. This includes flexible work hours, clear communication guidelines, and equitable access to opportunities. Companies like Zomato have introduced "period leave" and mental health days to support employee well-being.

3. **Building a Strong Remote Culture:** Creating a sense of belonging and connection in a virtual environment requires intentional efforts. Regular virtual meetings, recognition programs, and inclusive practices can help foster a strong organizational culture. For instance, Tata Steel has launched virtual mentorship programs to support employee growth and engagement.

4. **Upskilling Managers and Employees:** The transition to virtual and hybrid work requires new skills, such as digital

literacy, remote team management, and emotional intelligence. Organizations must invest in training programs to equip their workforce for success. A 2023 report by the World Economic Forum highlighted that 70% of Indian companies are prioritizing upskilling initiatives for their employees.

The Future of Virtual and Hybrid Work in India

The adoption of virtual and hybrid work models is not just a temporary trend but a fundamental shift in how work is organized and experienced. In India, this shift has the potential to drive economic growth, promote inclusivity, and enhance employee well-being. Nevertheless, its success will depend on the ability of organizations to address challenges and embrace innovation.

As we look toward the future, it is clear that virtual and hybrid work models are here to stay in India. According to a *2024 PwC India report*, 85% of Indian organizations are expected to adopt hybrid work models by 2026, with an emphasis on creating more flexible and employee-friendly work environments.

As we look to the future, virtual and hybrid organizations will continue to evolve, shaped by advancements in technology, changing employee expectations, and the need for sustainability. By prioritizing flexibility, collaboration, and inclusivity, Indian organizations can lead the way in redefining the future of work.

Case Studies of Indian Organizations

Infosys: One of India's largest IT companies, Infosys, has been a pioneer in adopting hybrid work models. The company introduced a "3x2" model where employees work from the office three days a week and have the flexibility to work remotely for the remaining two days. This model allows Infosys to balance the need for in-person collaboration with the flexibility of remote work. The company reported an increase in employee satisfaction and productivity as a result of this approach.

Tata Consultancy Services (TCS): TCS implemented a "Remote-First" approach, offering employees the option to work from home indefinitely. This shift was made possible due to the company's investment in cloud technologies and remote collaboration tools. TCS's move to a hybrid model was well-received, with employees appreciating the flexibility, while the company maintained its focus on client delivery through virtual collaborations.

Wipro: Another leading IT company in India, Wipro adopted a hybrid work model that encourages employees to work from home for three days a week, with the remaining two days dedicated to office work. This policy is part of the company's "Work Near Home" initiative, which aims to decentralize offices to reduce commuting and enhance work-life balance. This approach has proven effective in enhancing employee morale and increasing overall productivity.

4: RECRUITMENT STRATEGIES FOR MILLENNIALS AND GEN Z: ADAPTING TO THE NEW WORKFORCE DYNAMICS IN INDIA

Recruitment is the process of identifying, attracting, screening, selecting, and onboarding qualified candidates to fill organizational roles. It involves the strategic effort to find individuals who possess the necessary skills, qualifications, and cultural fit for the organization. Recruitment is a critical function in human resource management, as it directly impacts the organization's performance by ensuring a strong and capable workforce. The process encompasses various activities, including job postings, interviews, assessments, and negotiations, all aimed at securing the best talent available. The method of recruitment can vary depending on the organization's needs, ranging from traditional hiring practices to more advanced technology-driven approaches like recruitment through AI and social media platforms.

Author: Breaugh, J. A. (2008). Employee recruitment: Current knowledge and future directions. Human Resource Management Review, 18(3), 303-320.

The Indian workforce is undergoing a generational shift, with Millennials (born between 1981 and 1996) and Gen Z (born after 1997) now comprising a significant portion of the talent pool. By 2025, Millennials and Gen Z are expected to make up nearly 75% of India's workforce, according to a 2023 report by Deloitte India. This demographic transformation has profound implications for recruitment strategies, as these generations bring distinct values, expectations, and preferences to the workplace. This chapter explores the unique characteristics of Millennials and Gen Z, the challenges organizations face in recruiting them, and innovative strategies to attract and retain this new generation of talent in the Indian context.

Understanding Millennials and Gen Z

To design effective recruitment strategies, it is essential to understand what drives Millennials and Gen Z. While there are overlaps in their preferences, each generation has distinct traits that influence their career choices and workplace expectations.

Millennials: Often referred to as the "digital pioneers," Millennials value work-life balance, career growth opportunities, and a sense of purpose in their jobs. They are tech-savvy, collaborative, and seek meaningful connections with their employers. A 2023 survey by LinkedIn found that 68% of Indian Millennials prioritize organizations with strong learning and development programs.

Gen Z: The first true digital natives, Gen Z is characterized by their entrepreneurial spirit, desire for flexibility, and emphasis on diversity and inclusion. They are highly independent, value transparency, and are drawn to organizations that align with their personal values. A 2023 study by the Indian School of Business (ISB) revealed that 72% of Gen Z professionals in India prefer employers who demonstrate a commitment to social and environmental causes.

Challenges in Recruiting Millennials and Gen Z

Recruiting Millennials and Gen Z in India presents unique challenges for organizations:

High Expectations: Both generations have high expectations from their employers, including competitive salaries, opportunities for growth, and a positive workplace culture. A 2023 report by McKinsey India highlighted that 65% of Indian Millennials and Gen Z professionals are willing to switch jobs if their expectations are not met.

Digital-First Mindset: Millennials and Gen Z are accustomed to seamless digital experiences, and they expect the same from recruitment processes. Organizations that rely on outdated methods risk losing top talent to competitors with more tech-savvy approaches.

Diversity and Inclusion: Both generations place a strong emphasis on diversity, equity, and inclusion (DEI). A 2023 survey by NASSCOM found that 70% of Gen Z candidates in India consider an organization's DEI policies when evaluating job offers.

Retention Concerns: Attracting Millennials and Gen Z is only half the battle; retaining them is equally challenging. A 2023 study by the Society for Human Resource Management

(SHRM) India revealed that 60% of Indian organizations struggle with high attrition rates among younger employees.

Innovative Recruitment Strategies for Millennials and Gen Z

To attract and retain Millennials and Gen Z, Indian organizations must adopt innovative and tailored recruitment strategies:

1. **Leveraging Technology and Social Media:** Millennials and Gen Z are highly active on social media platforms like LinkedIn, Instagram, and YouTube. Organizations can use these platforms to showcase their employer brand, share employee stories, and engage with potential candidates. For example, companies like Zomato and Swiggy have successfully used social media campaigns to attract young talent by highlighting their vibrant workplace culture and employee benefits.

2. **Gamification in Recruitment:** Gamification is an effective way to engage Millennials and Gen Z, who enjoy interactive and immersive experiences. By incorporating gamified elements such as quizzes, challenges, and simulations into the recruitment process, organizations can make the experience more engaging and memorable. A 2023 study by the Indian Institute of Management (IIM) Bangalore found that gamified recruitment processes increased candidate engagement by 40%.

3. **Emphasizing Purpose and Values:** Millennials and Gen Z are drawn to organizations that align with their personal values and contribute to societal well-being. Highlighting corporate social responsibility (CSR) initiatives,

sustainability practices, and community impact can make an organization more attractive to these generations. For instance, Tata Group's "Tata Engage" program, which encourages employee volunteering, has been a key differentiator in attracting young talent.

4. **Flexible Work Arrangements:** Flexibility is a top priority for Millennials and Gen Z. Offering remote work options, flexible hours, and hybrid work models can give organizations a competitive edge. A 2023 report by KPMG India found that 80% of Indian professionals aged 18-35 prefer jobs that offer flexibility.

5. **Personalized Candidate Experiences:** Millennials and Gen Z expect personalized and transparent communication throughout the recruitment process. Using AI-driven tools to tailor job recommendations and provide real-time updates can enhance the candidate experience. Companies like Infosys and HCL Technologies have adopted AI-powered recruitment platforms to streamline hiring and improve candidate engagement.

6. **Focus on Learning and Development:** Both generations value continuous learning and career growth. Organizations that offer robust training programs, mentorship opportunities, and clear career progression paths are more likely to attract and retain young talent. For example, Wipro's "TopGear" initiative, which focuses on upskilling employees in emerging technologies, has been highly effective in engaging Millennials and Gen Z.

The Role of Innovative Recruitment Strategies in Indian Corporates: A Case Study Approach

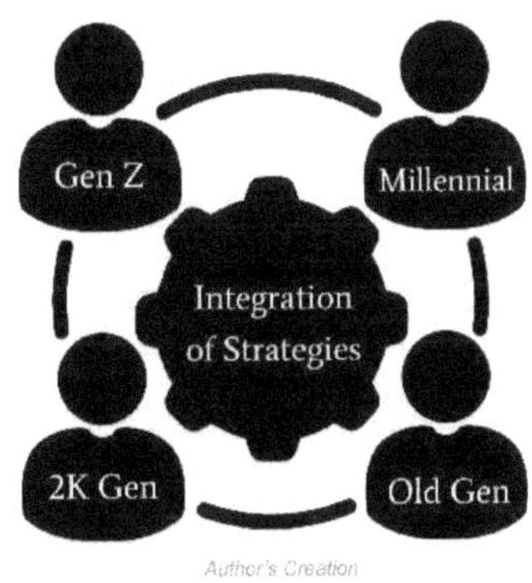

Author's Creation

In today's competitive business environment, attracting and retaining top talent has become one of the most critical challenges for organizations, particularly in India. With a rapidly evolving job market, companies must continually innovate to appeal to the diverse and dynamic workforce, especially younger generations such as Millennials and Gen Z, who are redefining expectations around work culture, career development, and organizational values. Several Indian organizations have successfully implemented unique recruitment strategies that not only meet these evolving demands but also position them as employers of choice. This section explores the recruitment strategies of three prominent Indian companies—Flipkart, Mahindra & Mahindra, and Byju's—highlighting how these organizations have leveraged innovative practices to attract top talent.

Flipkart, one of India's leading e-commerce giants, has emerged as a trailblazer in adopting a "candidate-first" approach to recruitment. In a world where candidates increasingly seek a seamless, engaging, and transparent hiring experience, Flipkart has leveraged cutting-edge technology, including artificial intelligence (AI) and social media platforms, to enhance its recruitment processes. The company's use of AI-driven tools to streamline candidate screening and matching ensures that the right candidates are identified quickly and efficiently. Over and above, Flipkart's recruitment process is designed to be engaging and responsive, with a focus on providing candidates with timely feedback and clear communication at every stage. This approach reflects the company's deep commitment to innovation and its recognition that the recruitment process is not just about finding the right skills but also about creating a positive experience for candidates. For Flipkart, recruitment is seen as a two-way relationship, where they not only assess candidates but also work to build their employer brand in the eyes of potential hires. The company's emphasis on empowerment and creativity has made it a top choice for young professionals, particularly those seeking opportunities in the fast-paced and ever-evolving tech and e-commerce sectors.

Mahindra & Mahindra, a global leader in the automotive and agricultural sectors, has long been recognized for its strong employer brand. The company has been particularly successful in attracting Millennials and Gen Z talent by emphasizing its commitment to sustainability, social responsibility, and the greater good. One of the key aspects of Mahindra & Mahindra's recruitment strategy is its "Rise" philosophy, which underscores the company's core values of innovation, leadership, and sustainability. This philosophy resonates deeply with younger generations, who are increasingly motivated by a sense of purpose and a desire to contribute to causes that align with their personal values. The company's emphasis on social impact, sustainability, and ethical business practices appeals to a growing segment of candidates who seek meaningful work that goes beyond profit generation. Through various campaigns and initiatives, Mahindra & Mahindra has effectively communicated its brand as an employer that fosters a culture of growth, empowerment, and responsibility, positioning itself as an organization where employees can make a difference, both professionally and socially. By emphasizing these values in its recruitment messaging, Mahindra & Mahindra has successfully attracted a diverse pool of talent that shares the company's commitment to social impact and sustainable business practices.

Byju's, India's leading edtech company, has adopted a highly engaging and interactive recruitment process that aligns with the company's focus on innovation and learning. Recognizing that younger generations, especially Millennials and Gen Z, prefer interactive and gamified experiences, Byju's has integrated gamification into its recruitment process to make it more engaging and enjoyable for candidates. Byju's recruitment process often includes real-world problem-solving tasks and interactive challenges that test candidates' analytical thinking, creativity, and problem-solving abilities. This approach not only gives candidates a clear understanding of the skills required for the role but also creates an opportunity for them to experience firsthand what it might be like to work at Byju's. The gamified recruitment process reflects Byju's commitment to learning and development, a core value of the company that resonates strongly with the younger workforce, who are eager for continuous growth and learning opportunities. Over and above, Byju's emphasis on learning and skill-building, both for its employees and its customers, is a key factor that has helped the company attract young talent looking for meaningful and growth-oriented careers in the dynamic edtech space.

These three companies—Flipkart, Mahindra & Mahindra, and Byju's—have demonstrated the power of innovation in recruitment, each using a unique approach to align their hiring practices with the expectations and values of today's workforce. Flipkart's use of AI and social media to create a candidate-first experience reflects its commitment to providing a seamless and engaging recruitment journey. Mahindra & Mahindra's focus on sustainability, social impact, and the "Rise" philosophy resonates deeply with younger generations who are driven by purpose-driven work. Byju's, with its gamified recruitment process, creates an interactive and immersive experience that appeals to candidates looking for dynamic and innovative roles in the fast-growing edtech sector.

These companies have recognized that attracting top talent today requires more than just a competitive salary or traditional job perks. They have adopted forward-thinking recruitment strategies that cater to the evolving preferences of the new workforce. For HR professionals, management students, and OB experts, understanding the recruitment strategies of these organizations provides valuable insights into the changing landscape of talent acquisition in India. As organizations continue to navigate the challenges of attracting, engaging, and retaining top talent, the focus must shift from traditional recruitment methods to more innovative, flexible, and candidate-centric approaches that emphasize personalization, transparency, and alignment with employees' values and career aspirations.

For all that Flipkart, Mahindra & Mahindra, and Byju's serve as exemplary models of how Indian organizations can adapt their recruitment practices to meet the needs and expectations of the modern workforce. By leveraging technology, emphasizing social impact, and creating engaging experiences, these companies have successfully positioned themselves as employers of choice for young professionals. As the Indian job market continues to evolve, organizations that embrace innovation in their recruitment processes will be better equipped to attract, develop, and retain the talent necessary to drive future growth and success.

Recruiting Millennials and Gen Z in India requires a paradigm shift in how organizations approach talent acquisition. By understanding the unique values and preferences of these generations, leveraging technology, and emphasizing purpose and flexibility, organizations can build a strong employer brand and attract top talent. The future of work belongs to those who can adapt to the evolving expectations of the workforce, and Indian organizations have a unique opportunity to lead the way in redefining recruitment strategies for the new generation.

---

5. AI IN HIRING: TOOLS AND TECHNIQUES TRANSFORMING RECRUITMENT IN INDIA

Recruitment is the process by which organizations identify, attract, and select candidates to fill vacancies within their workforce. It involves a series of strategic actions aimed at finding and hiring individuals with the necessary skills, qualifications, and cultural fit for specific roles in the organization. Recruitment is often seen as a key function in Human Resource Management (HRM) because it directly impacts the organization's ability to achieve its goals through the talent it brings on board. The process can range from traditional methods such as job advertisements and interviews to modern, technology-driven approaches involving social media platforms, artificial intelligence (AI), and recruitment software.

Author: Armstrong, M. (2006). A Handbook of Human Resource Management Practice. Kogan Page.

The recruitment landscape in India is undergoing a profound transformation, driven by the rapid adoption of Artificial Intelligence (AI). As organizations grapple with the challenges of attracting top talent in a competitive market, AI-powered tools and techniques are emerging as game-changers, enabling faster, smarter, and more efficient hiring processes. From automating repetitive tasks to enhancing candidate experiences, AI is reshaping every aspect of recruitment. This chapter explores the role of AI in hiring, the tools and techniques being used in Indian organizations, and the implications for recruiters and candidates alike.

The Rise of AI in Recruitment: Transforming Talent Acquisition in Indian Organizations

The recruitment landscape in India has undergone a remarkable transformation in recent years, driven by

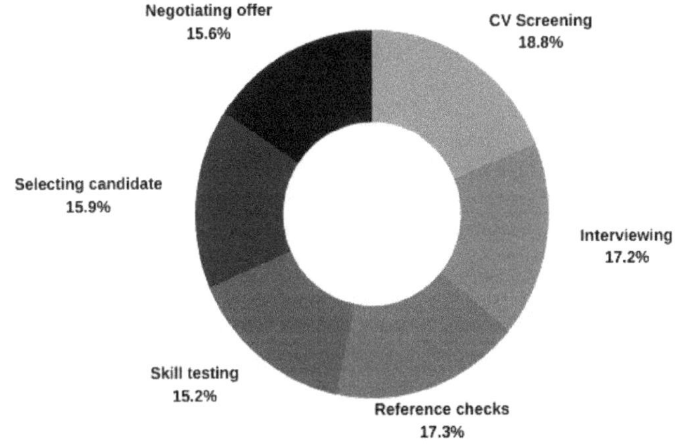

Source: Robert Half UK

advancements in technology, with Artificial Intelligence (AI) emerging as one of the most significant disruptors. As organizations face increasing pressure to attract and retain top talent in an ever-competitive job market, AI has become a powerful tool that is reshaping the way companies approach talent acquisition. From automating repetitive tasks to enhancing the candidate experience, AI is playing a pivotal role in streamlining and optimizing the recruitment process for Indian organizations across various industries.

In the past, recruitment was primarily a manual process, with HR professionals relying on resumes, interviews, and basic assessments to evaluate candidates. While this method served its purpose, it was often time-consuming, prone to bias, and limited in its ability to evaluate candidates holistically. With the rise of AI, these traditional methods are being replaced with more sophisticated, data-driven approaches that enable HR professionals to make more informed, objective, and efficient hiring decisions. AI-powered recruitment tools can quickly sift through large volumes of resumes, matching candidates' qualifications, skills, and experiences with the requirements of the job, thereby reducing the burden of manual screening.

One of the most notable applications of AI in recruitment is in the automation of candidate sourcing and screening. Indian companies, especially those in the IT, e-commerce, and manufacturing sectors, are increasingly using AI algorithms to identify and engage potential candidates from a pool of talent. Platforms like LinkedIn, Naukri, and Indeed have integrated AI into their systems to help companies find the right talent faster and more effectively. AI tools are capable of parsing resumes and application forms to identify key skills, experiences, and qualifications that align with the job description. This reduces the time spent on manual resume review and allows HR professionals to focus on more strategic aspects of recruitment, such as candidate engagement and organizational fit.

AI is also helping organizations mitigate unconscious bias in the hiring process. Traditional recruitment processes can sometimes be influenced by human biases related to gender, age, ethnicity, or educational background, which may lead to less diverse hiring decisions. AI-powered systems can be designed to ignore demographic data, focusing instead on the skills, experience, and qualifications of candidates. By removing this potential for bias, AI can help companies make more equitable and inclusive hiring decisions, leading to greater diversity in the workforce. This is particularly important in the context of Indian organizations, where diversity—across gender, caste, region, and educational background—is an essential component of organizational growth and innovation.

Some other critical area where AI is making a difference in recruitment is in enhancing the candidate experience. Indian organizations are increasingly adopting AI-powered chatbots and virtual assistants to engage with candidates at various stages of the hiring process. These AI tools can provide immediate responses to candidate queries, schedule interviews, send follow-up emails, and even guide candidates through the application process. This not only improves the efficiency of the recruitment process but also provides candidates with a seamless, responsive experience, which can enhance their perception of the employer brand. Companies like Tata Consultancy Services (TCS) and Infosys are already utilizing AI-driven chatbots to interact with candidates and provide them with personalized updates, creating a more engaging and transparent hiring journey.

AI is also playing a pivotal role in predictive analytics, helping organizations forecast the success of a candidate in a given role. By analyzing historical data on employee performance, AI algorithms can identify patterns and traits that are associated with high performers. This data-driven approach enables organizations to make more informed hiring decisions by predicting which candidates are most likely to succeed in the role. For instance, AI tools can analyze factors such as cultural fit, work ethic, and past performance to assess whether a candidate will thrive in the organization's environment. This is particularly useful in Indian organizations, where employee retention is a significant concern, and finding the right cultural fit is essential to ensuring long-term success.

The application of AI in recruitment is not limited to just large organizations. Startups and small-to-medium-sized enterprises (SMEs) in India are also increasingly leveraging AI to streamline their hiring processes. For smaller companies with limited HR resources, AI offers an affordable and efficient way to compete with larger firms in the battle for top talent. AI-powered platforms provide SMEs with the ability to access a larger pool of candidates, automate routine tasks, and make more data-driven decisions, leveling the playing field and allowing them to attract skilled professionals without the need for a large, in-house recruitment team.

As AI continues to evolve, its capabilities in recruitment are expanding. One of the exciting developments is the use of AI in assessing soft skills, such as communication, teamwork, and emotional intelligence. Traditional recruitment methods primarily focus on evaluating technical skills and qualifications, but soft skills are increasingly recognized as critical for success in today's workplace. AI tools are now being developed to analyze candidates' interactions in interviews, their social media profiles, and even their responses to behavioral assessments to gain deeper insights into their emotional intelligence and interpersonal abilities. This holistic approach to candidate evaluation is especially important for Indian organizations, where a strong emphasis on collaboration, team dynamics, and leadership is central to organizational success.

Even if the significant advantages AI brings to the recruitment process, it is important to recognize that it is not without its challenges. The widespread adoption of AI in recruitment has raised concerns about the potential for job displacement, particularly in traditional HR roles. While AI can automate many aspects of recruitment, the role of human judgment and empathy remains crucial, especially in areas such as final interviews, negotiation, and cultural fit assessment. HR professionals in India must, therefore, find ways to integrate AI into their processes while ensuring that human intuition and decision-making are not overshadowed by automation.

Considering the implementation of AI in recruitment must be done with caution, ensuring that algorithms are transparent, ethical, and free from biases. While AI has the potential to reduce human biases, if not carefully designed, it can perpetuate existing biases in the data it is trained on. For Indian organizations, this means ensuring that AI systems are regularly monitored and updated to reflect changing societal norms and values, particularly in areas like gender and caste diversity.

As AI continues to reshape the recruitment landscape in India, it presents significant opportunities for HR professionals and organizations to optimize their talent acquisition processes. By leveraging AI tools to enhance candidate sourcing, reduce bias, improve the candidate experience, and predict success, Indian organizations can create a more efficient, inclusive, and data-driven recruitment process. Though, it is essential for HR professionals to strike a balance between automation and human interaction, ensuring that AI serves as a tool to complement, rather than replace, the human element in recruitment. As AI continues to advance, its role in recruitment will only grow, and organizations that embrace this technology will be better positioned to attract and retain top talent in an increasingly competitive market.

Key AI Tools and Techniques in Hiring: Transforming Recruitment in Indian Organizations

As the demand for top talent intensifies across industries in India, organizations are increasingly turning to Artificial Intelligence (AI) to enhance their recruitment processes. The integration of AI tools and techniques has not only streamlined various stages of hiring but has also enabled Indian companies to reduce time-to-hire, improve the quality of hires, and foster a more inclusive and diverse workforce. From automating mundane tasks like resume screening to leveraging predictive analytics for talent acquisition, AI is revolutionizing the way organizations approach recruitment.

One of the most prominent AI tools in recruitment is AI-powered resume screening and candidate sourcing. Tools like HireVue and Hiretual use machine learning algorithms to analyze resumes by comparing them against predefined criteria, such as job-specific skills, experiences, and qualifications. These tools can quickly scan thousands of resumes in a matter of minutes, significantly reducing the time and effort involved in manual screening. For Indian organizations, where the volume of applications can be overwhelming, these AI tools provide a much-needed solution to filter out unqualified candidates and identify those who are the best fit for the role. Tata Consultancy Services (TCS), for instance, has successfully implemented an AI-driven resume screening system that has reduced its hiring cycle by approximately 30%. By using AI to automate the resume review process, TCS has not only sped up recruitment but also improved the overall efficiency of its hiring operations.

An alternative AI tool making waves in Indian recruitment is the AI-powered chatbot. Platforms like Mya and XOR are being used by companies to engage with candidates throughout the recruitment process. These chatbots provide a more personalized experience by answering candidate queries, offering guidance on the application process, and ensuring that candidates remain informed at every stage. The use of chatbots has proven to be particularly effective in maintaining candidate engagement, which can often be a challenge in lengthy recruitment processes. According to a 2023 study by Deloitte India, organizations that adopted AI chatbots reported a 40% improvement in candidate satisfaction. For HR professionals, chatbots help alleviate the burden of responding to repetitive queries, allowing them to focus on more strategic tasks such as candidate evaluation and decision-making.

Barring to chatbots, AI is also transforming the way interviews are conducted, particularly through video interviewing and facial analysis. Platforms like HireVue and Pymetrics use AI to analyze video interviews by evaluating candidates' facial expressions, tone of voice, and language patterns. This technology helps to assess not only the technical skills of candidates but also their soft skills, such as emotional intelligence and communication abilities, which are crucial for many roles in today's workplace. The banking and IT sectors in India have been early adopters of this technology, with companies like HDFC Bank using AI-powered video interviewing to evaluate candidates' cultural fit and interpersonal skills. This approach allows for a more objective assessment of candidates' suitability for a role, minimizing the potential for unconscious bias that can occur in traditional face-to-face interviews.

AI-driven skill assessments and gamification are also gaining traction in the Indian recruitment landscape. Tools like Mercer Mettl and Codility use gamified assessments and real-world simulations to evaluate candidates' technical abilities and cognitive skills. These tools provide a more engaging and standardized approach to assessing candidates, ensuring that the evaluation process is both objective and fair. By using AI to administer assessments that mimic real-world challenges, organizations can gain deeper insights into candidates' problem-solving skills, creativity, and ability to perform under pressure. The use of gamification also appeals to younger generations, particularly Millennials and Gen Z, who value interactive and engaging experiences. A 2023 report by the Indian Institute of Management (IIM) Ahmedabad revealed that organizations using AI-based assessments saw a 25% increase in the quality of hires. For Indian organizations, this means a more reliable and accurate way to assess candidates' capabilities before making hiring decisions.

Predictive analytics, powered by AI, is another tool that is helping Indian companies optimize their recruitment strategies. AI-powered predictive analytics tools analyze historical data to forecast hiring needs, identify high-potential candidates, and predict their likelihood of success in a particular role. Companies like Infosys and Wipro have been using predictive analytics to build talent pipelines and reduce time-to-hire by identifying candidates who are most likely to succeed within the organization. By leveraging AI to predict future talent needs and success rates, these companies can proactively engage with candidates, ensuring that they have a steady stream of qualified talent ready to fill open positions. According to a 2023 study by McKinsey India, organizations using predictive analytics saw a 20% improvement in recruitment efficiency, as these tools enabled them to make data-driven decisions that significantly reduced the time and effort spent on sourcing and evaluating candidates.

Bias reduction and diversity hiring are other areas where AI is making a substantial impact in Indian recruitment practices. Unconscious bias in the hiring process can lead to discrimination, particularly when it comes to gender, age, ethnicity, or educational background. AI tools are being designed to minimize these biases by focusing on objective criteria such as skills, qualifications, and experience, rather than subjective factors. For example, AI algorithms can anonymize resumes by removing demographic details like names, gender, and age, ensuring that the evaluation process remains fair and impartial. According to a 2023 survey by LinkedIn, 55% of Indian organizations reported using AI to promote diversity and inclusion in their hiring processes. By using AI to promote a more unbiased and inclusive recruitment process, Indian companies are able to attract a more diverse pool of candidates, which is essential for fostering innovation and building high-performing teams.

Along with the advantages that AI tools bring to recruitment, Indian organizations must also be mindful of the challenges that come with implementing these technologies. One of the key concerns is the potential for AI systems to perpetuate existing biases if they are not designed and monitored carefully. AI systems are only as good as the data they are trained on, and if this data contains biases, the algorithms may reinforce those biases in the hiring process. That being the case, it is essential for HR professionals to ensure that AI systems are regularly audited and updated to ensure fairness and transparency. Too, while AI can streamline many aspects of recruitment, the human touch remains essential in areas such as final interviews and cultural fit assessments, where empathy, intuition, and judgment are still critical.

Benefits of AI in Hiring

The adoption of AI in recruitment offers several benefits for Indian organizations:

Efficiency and Speed: AI automates repetitive tasks, enabling recruiters to process applications faster and focus on strategic activities. A 2023 report by KPMG India found that AI reduced the average time-to-hire by 35% in Indian organizations.

Improved Candidate Experience: AI-powered chatbots and personalized communication tools enhance the candidate experience by providing timely updates and addressing queries promptly.

Data-Driven Decisions: AI provides actionable insights based on data, helping recruiters make informed decisions and improve the quality of hires.

Cost Savings: By automating manual processes, AI reduces recruitment costs and improves return on investment (ROI).

Challenges and Ethical Considerations

While AI offers significant advantages, its adoption in recruitment is not without challenges:

1. **Bias in AI Algorithms:** If not designed carefully, AI tools can perpetuate existing biases in the data they are trained on. For example, an AI system trained on historical hiring data may favor certain demographics over others.

2. **Lack of Human Touch:** Over-reliance on AI can lead to a lack of personal interaction, which is crucial for building relationships with candidates.

3. **Data Privacy Concerns:** The use of AI in recruitment raises concerns about data privacy and security,

particularly in a country like India where data protection laws are still evolving.

4. **Skill Gaps:** Implementing AI tools requires specialized skills, and many Indian organizations struggle with a lack of expertise in AI and data analytics.

Case Studies: AI in Hiring in Indian Organizations

Several Indian organizations have successfully integrated AI into their recruitment processes:

Infosys: The IT giant has developed an AI-powered recruitment platform called "InfyTQ," which assesses candidates' technical skills and provides personalized learning paths. This initiative has helped Infosys identify and nurture top talent.

Byju's: The edtech leader uses AI-driven assessments and gamification to evaluate candidates' problem-solving abilities and cultural fit. Byju's has reported a 30% improvement in hiring efficiency since adopting AI tools.

Axis Bank: The bank has implemented an AI chatbot called "Aha!" to engage with candidates and streamline the application process. This has resulted in a 50% reduction in candidate drop-off rates.

---

6. THE ROLE OF AI, ML, AND BLOCKCHAIN IN HR: TRANSFORMING HUMAN RESOURCE MANAGEMENT IN INDIA

Human Resources (HR) refers to the strategic approach to the management of an organization's most valuable asset—its people. HR encompasses a wide range of functions, including recruitment, training and development, performance management, compensation, benefits, employee relations, and organizational development. The goal of HR is to ensure that the organization has the right people in place to meet its objectives and to create a supportive environment that allows employees to thrive and perform to the best of their abilities. HR plays a pivotal role in shaping organizational culture and aligning human capital with business strategies.

Author: Dessler, G. (2017). Human Resource Management (15th ed.). Pearson.

The Human Resources (HR) function is no longer confined to administrative tasks and employee management. In the digital age, HR has evolved into a strategic powerhouse, leveraging cutting-edge technologies like Artificial

Intelligence (AI), Machine Learning (ML), and Blockchain to drive organizational success. These technologies are revolutionizing HR practices in India, enabling organizations to enhance efficiency, improve decision-making, and create a more engaging and transparent workplace. This chapter explores the transformative role of AI, ML, and Blockchain in HR, with a focus on their applications, benefits, and challenges in the Indian context.

AI-Driven Recruitment: Revolutionizing Hiring in Indian Organizations

The landscape of recruitment in Indian organizations is undergoing a fundamental transformation, driven by the integration of Artificial Intelligence (AI) technologies. As businesses in India face the dual challenges of a rapidly changing job market and an increasingly competitive talent pool, AI has emerged as a powerful tool to enhance the recruitment process, enabling companies to streamline operations, reduce time-to-hire, and improve the quality of their hires.

AI-driven recruitment leverages machine learning, natural language processing, and other advanced technologies to automate and optimize various stages of the hiring process. From sourcing and screening candidates to conducting interviews and assessments, AI is redefining how organizations identify, evaluate, and select talent. This shift is particularly significant in India, where a large and diverse pool of job seekers, combined with the country's fast-paced digital transformation, presents unique opportunities for leveraging AI in recruitment.

One of the most prominent applications of AI in recruitment is in resume screening and candidate sourcing. Habitually, HR professionals would spend hours manually sifting through resumes, identifying suitable candidates based on their qualifications, experience, and skills. AI-powered tools like HireVue, Hiretual, and X0R have drastically reduced this workload by automating the screening process. These tools use machine learning algorithms to scan resumes, match them to job descriptions, and identify candidates that best meet the requirements. For Indian companies, where a single job opening can attract hundreds, if not thousands, of applications, AI offers a much-needed solution to efficiently filter candidates. Large organizations such as Tata Consultancy Services (TCS) have implemented AI-driven resume screening systems, resulting in faster recruitment cycles and significantly less manual intervention.

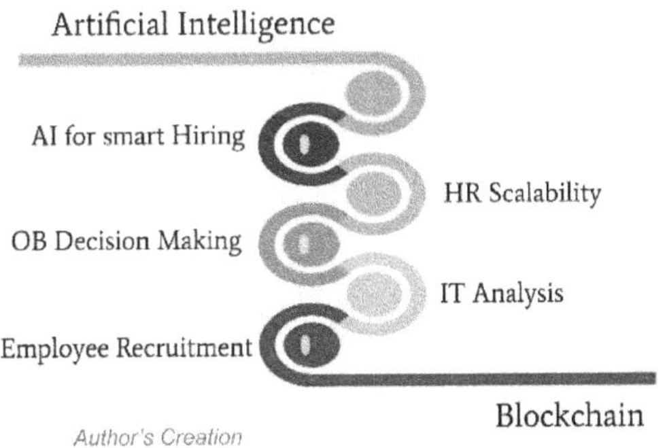

In excess to resume screening, AI is also transforming candidate engagement. Chatbots powered by AI, such as Mya and X0R, are being increasingly used to interact with candidates during the hiring process. These chatbots can answer frequently asked questions, guide candidates through the application process, and provide instant feedback on their application status. For candidates, the experience is seamless and personalized, allowing them to engage with the organization without delay. For HR professionals, AI chatbots streamline candidate engagement, reducing the time spent answering repetitive queries and freeing up valuable resources to focus on more strategic tasks. A 2023 study by Deloitte India found that organizations using AI chatbots reported a 40% improvement in candidate satisfaction, indicating the value these tools bring to the recruitment experience.

Video interviewing powered by AI has also gained significant traction in India, particularly in sectors like banking, IT, and retail, where speed and efficiency are critical. Platforms such as HireVue and Pymetrics use AI to analyze video interviews, assessing candidates' facial expressions, body language, tone of voice, and language patterns to evaluate their suitability for a role. This technology allows HR professionals to assess candidates more comprehensively, including their soft skills and cultural fit, which are often difficult to evaluate through traditional means. In organizations like HDFC Bank and ICICI Bank, AI-powered video interviews have become an integral part of their hiring process, allowing them to assess candidates' interpersonal skills and emotional intelligence more effectively. These platforms also help eliminate bias by focusing on objective data points, such as speech patterns and non-verbal cues, rather than relying on human judgment alone.

Beyond resume screening and video interviews, AI is also reshaping the way Indian companies assess candidates' technical and cognitive abilities. AI-powered skill assessments, including gamified platforms like Mercer Mettl and Codility, have become essential tools for evaluating candidates in a standardized and objective manner. These tools simulate real-world scenarios and challenges to assess problem-solving skills, logical thinking, and technical knowledge. Gamification, which appeals to younger generations, particularly Millennials and Gen Z, is a growing trend in recruitment. By making assessments more engaging and interactive, AI-driven gamification ensures that candidates are evaluated in a way that mirrors the demands of the job. For example, companies in the IT sector, such as Wipro and Infosys, use AI-driven assessments to evaluate candidates' coding abilities or problem-solving skills, ensuring that they select the most capable talent. According to a report by the Indian Institute of Management (IIM) Ahmedabad, organizations using AI-based assessments saw a 25% increase in the quality of their hires, as these tools offered a more accurate and objective evaluation compared to traditional methods.

One more significant application of AI in recruitment is predictive analytics. Predictive analytics tools use historical data to forecast future talent needs, identify high-potential candidates, and predict their likelihood of success in a given role. These tools analyze patterns in hiring data, such as previous hiring decisions, employee performance, and retention rates, to make data-driven predictions. Companies like Infosys and Wipro have successfully implemented AI-driven predictive analytics to anticipate their hiring needs, build talent pipelines, and reduce time-to-hire. For instance, by analyzing historical data, these organizations can predict when their workforce will require new talent and proactively engage with candidates, ensuring that they are ready to fill open positions quickly and effectively. McKinsey India's 2023 study showed that organizations using predictive analytics in recruitment saw a 20% improvement in efficiency, demonstrating the significant impact this technology can have on recruitment outcomes.

AI's ability to reduce bias and promote diversity in recruitment is another key benefit for Indian organizations. In a country as diverse as India, where biases related to gender, caste, and socioeconomic background are often prevalent in hiring decisions, AI offers a more impartial approach. By removing demographic details such as names, gender, and age from resumes, AI algorithms can focus solely on candidates' qualifications, experience, and skills. AI also helps identify and eliminate unconscious bias by ensuring that the recruitment process is based on objective, data-driven criteria. According to a LinkedIn survey, 55% of Indian organizations have used AI tools to promote diversity and inclusion in hiring. This is particularly important for organizations aiming to create diverse and inclusive workplaces, which are known to foster innovation and improve team performance.

There are many benefits, AI-driven recruitment also presents challenges for Indian organizations. One of the key concerns is the risk of perpetuating existing biases in the algorithms themselves. AI tools are trained using historical data, which may contain biases reflecting societal inequalities. If not carefully managed, these biases can be replicated and reinforced by AI, potentially undermining efforts to promote diversity and inclusion. That being the case, it is crucial for HR professionals to regularly audit AI systems to ensure they are fair and transparent in their decision-making processes.

Hence, while AI can automate many aspects of recruitment, human judgment remains essential in certain areas, particularly when it comes to assessing candidates' cultural fit, interpersonal skills, and alignment with the organization's values. While AI can provide valuable insights, it cannot replace the emotional intelligence and intuition that human recruiters bring to the table. As such, a hybrid approach, combining AI-driven automation with human decision-making, is often the most effective way to ensure that recruitment decisions are both data-driven and empathetic.

Performance Management and Employee Analytics: Transforming HR Practices with AI and ML in Indian Organizations

The traditional approach to performance management in Indian organizations has long been criticized for its subjectivity, bias, and inconsistency. Historically, performance reviews were often based on managers' perceptions, with limited data-driven insights. Feedback was typically one-sided, and the process lacked regularity and transparency. Although, the introduction of Artificial Intelligence (AI) and Machine Learning (ML) is revolutionizing the performance management landscape by offering more objective, real-time, and data-driven approaches that enable HR professionals to gain deeper insights into employee performance.

AI and ML play a pivotal role in transforming performance management by allowing organizations to monitor employee performance continuously and in real time. For instance, AI-powered tools such as KPI Builder and ADP Workforce Now are increasingly being adopted by Indian organizations to track key performance indicators (KPIs), productivity, and peer feedback. These tools provide a more comprehensive and accurate picture of employee performance by gathering data from various sources and analyzing it systematically. Instead of relying solely on periodic performance reviews, AI systems enable HR professionals to access real-time data, helping to identify high performers, flag potential underperformers, and make informed decisions about talent development.

AI's ability to offer objective and continuous insights into performance is a game changer. In a country like India, where a large proportion of the workforce is employed in fast-paced sectors such as IT, manufacturing, and services, performance management needs to be agile and responsive. With AI, organizations can not only track how employees are performing relative to predefined goals but also gain deeper insights into the factors contributing to their success or areas that need improvement. AI tools can predict future performance trends by analyzing historical data and identifying patterns that may have been overlooked in traditional systems. For example, ML algorithms can pinpoint factors such as workload balance, team dynamics, or training deficiencies that influence an employee's performance trajectory. This level of insight helps managers provide more precise feedback, offer targeted interventions, and ultimately improve employee outcomes.

Comparatively, AI-powered sentiment analysis tools, such as those employed by companies like Wipro and Infosys, are enhancing the way Indian organizations assess employee engagement. These tools process employee surveys, feedback forms, and other communication data to gauge workforce sentiment. Sentiment analysis helps HR departments track employee mood, job satisfaction, and alignment with the company's values and goals. By understanding employees' emotions and motivations, HR leaders can make data-driven decisions to improve organizational culture and address specific concerns, such as work-life balance, leadership effectiveness, or team collaboration. This shift to data-driven decision-making, facilitated by AI, allows organizations to be more responsive and proactive in addressing employee needs, ultimately fostering a more engaged and productive workforce.

The benefits of AI-driven performance management are tangible, particularly in terms of productivity. A 2023 report by Accenture India found that organizations using AI and ML-based performance management systems saw a 40% increase in employee productivity compared to those relying on traditional methods. This significant improvement is attributed to the ability of AI systems to continuously monitor performance, offer personalized feedback, and make real-time adjustments. With AI, Indian organizations can ensure that their workforce remains engaged, motivated, and on track to meet organizational goals.

Not the same critical area where AI and ML are making an impact is in Learning and Development (L&D). In the past, L&D programs in many organizations followed a one-size-fits-all approach, where employees were provided with generic training content. That being the case, with AI-driven platforms, companies can now offer more personalized and dynamic learning experiences tailored to the individual needs, preferences, and career goals of each employee. Leading Indian companies such as Zee Entertainment and Reliance Industries are leveraging AI-powered platforms like LinkedIn Learning and EdCast to recommend customized training programs to employees. These platforms use algorithms to analyze an employee's past performance, current skill set, and career aspirations, providing targeted recommendations for learning content that aligns with their personal development goals.

Machine learning further enhances L&D by continuously analyzing an employee's progress and adjusting the training content accordingly. For example, if an employee is excelling in a specific area, the platform can adjust the learning path to introduce more advanced material. Conversely, if an employee is struggling with a particular concept, the system can provide additional resources or simplify the content to ensure mastery of the topic. This adaptive learning approach ensures that employees receive the most relevant training at the right time, enhancing their skill development and helping them progress along their career path.

As a result, AI and ML are making L&D programs more forward-looking by predicting which skills will be most valuable in the future. In a rapidly changing business environment like India's, where technological advancements are transforming industries, companies must be proactive in ensuring that their workforce remains competitive. AI-powered systems analyze industry trends, organizational needs, and employee performance data to predict the skills that will be in demand in the coming years. This enables HR departments to design training programs that equip employees with the skills they will need in the future, helping both the individual and the organization stay ahead of the curve.

The dynamic capabilities of AI in performance management and L&D are empowering HR departments in Indian organizations to not only optimize current performance but also to build a more agile, skilled, and future-ready workforce. By embracing these technologies, companies can foster a culture of continuous learning, increase employee satisfaction, and ultimately improve business outcomes. AI and ML are not just transforming how performance is managed, but also how organizations approach talent development, making them indispensable tools for driving organizational success in the modern business environment.

Blockchain in HR: Enhancing Transparency, Security, and Efficiency

Blockchain technology, often associated with cryptocurrency, has broader applications in HR, particularly in areas requiring secure and transparent data management. Indian organizations are increasingly leveraging blockchain to address issues related to data privacy, employee verification, and contract management.

1. Smart Contracts and Payroll Management

Blockchain's ability to create smart contracts has significant implications for HR departments. A smart contract is a self-executing contract with the terms of the agreement directly written into lines of code. This ensures that both parties fulfill their obligations automatically without requiring intermediaries.

For example, companies like *HCL Technologies* and *Mahindra Group* are exploring blockchain to streamline payroll processes. Blockchain ensures that employees' compensation, bonuses, and incentives are processed with high levels of accuracy, transparency, and security. By reducing the potential for fraud or errors in payroll calculations, blockchain ensures that employees are paid promptly and accurately.

Again, blockchain enables real-time tracking of payroll transactions, providing employees with the ability to verify their earnings and deductions, ensuring complete transparency in the payment process. This reduces disputes and increases employee trust.

2. Secure Employee Records and Identity Verification

Blockchain is increasingly being used to manage employee records securely. Generally, managing employee data, including academic qualifications, certifications, work history, and performance records, has been cumbersome and prone to data breaches.

Blockchain, however, allows organizations to store employee data in a decentralized and tamper-proof manner. *ICICI*

Bank, for example, has adopted blockchain to store employee verification records, such as academic qualifications and employment history. The use of blockchain guarantees that this data cannot be altered or manipulated, ensuring the authenticity of employee credentials.

Thus, blockchain is being used to streamline employee onboarding. New employees can securely upload their documents to a blockchain ledger, which can then be accessed by HR departments for verification. This eliminates the need for manual verification and accelerates the hiring process.

3. Enhancing Employee Benefits and Leave Management

Blockchain's transparency and immutability can also be applied to the management of employee benefits, including insurance, retirement funds, and leave management. By using blockchain, organizations can automate the administration of these benefits, ensuring accuracy and reducing administrative overheads.

For instance, *L&T Group* has experimented with blockchain for handling employee leave records, ensuring that each employee's leave balance is accurately tracked and stored in a decentralized ledger, reducing the chances of errors or discrepancies.

Benefits of AI, ML, and Blockchain in HR

The integration of AI, ML, and Blockchain into HR offers several benefits for Indian organizations:

Improved Efficiency: Automation of repetitive tasks frees up HR professionals to focus on strategic initiatives.

Enhanced Decision-Making: Data-driven insights enable HR teams to make informed decisions and improve outcomes.

Better Employee Experiences: Personalized and transparent processes enhance employee satisfaction and engagement.

Increased Security: Blockchain ensures the integrity and security of sensitive HR data.

Challenges and Ethical Considerations

Along side their potential, the adoption of AI, ML, and Blockchain in HR is not without challenges:

Data Privacy Concerns: The use of these technologies raises concerns about data privacy and security, particularly in India where data protection laws are still evolving. HR departments must ensure that AI and Blockchain systems comply with data protection regulations such as the *Personal Data Protection Bill, 2019* in India.

Bias in AI Algorithms: If not designed carefully, AI and ML systems can perpetuate existing biases in the data they are trained on. If these algorithms are not properly managed, they may inadvertently perpetuate biases, leading to discrimination in recruitment or performance evaluation.

High Implementation Costs: The initial investment required for implementing these technologies can be prohibitive for small and medium-sized enterprises (SMEs). The cost of acquiring the technology and training HR staff can be significant, and the time taken to integrate these solutions into existing systems may be considerable.

Skill Gaps: The successful implementation of AI, ML, and Blockchain requires specialized skills, which are often in short supply. Over and above, there may be resistance to change among employees and managers who are accustomed to traditional HR processes.

The Future of HR with AI, ML, and Blockchain

The future of HR in India is set to be increasingly shaped by AI, ML, and Blockchain technologies. As more organizations adopt these tools, HR processes will become more automated, personalized, and data-driven. AI and ML will continue to enhance recruitment, performance management, and employee engagement, while blockchain will ensure greater transparency, security, and efficiency in payroll and employee record management.

The next frontier will involve integrating these technologies with emerging trends like Augmented Reality (AR) and Virtual Reality (VR) for immersive training experiences and further enhancing the employee experience.

Case Studies: AI, ML, and Blockchain in Indian Organizations

Several Indian organizations have successfully leveraged these technologies to transform their HR functions:

TCS: The IT giant has implemented an AI-driven recruitment platform that has reduced hiring time by 30% and improved the quality of hires.

Wipro: The company uses AI to monitor employee sentiment and predict attrition risks, enabling proactive retention strategies.

Mahindra & Mahindra: The automotive leader is exploring Blockchain for credential verification and payroll management, ensuring transparency and compliance.

As author mentioned earlier, AI, ML, and Blockchain are reshaping the HR landscape in India, offering unprecedented opportunities to enhance efficiency, transparency, and employee experiences. Anyhow, their successful implementation requires a strategic approach that addresses challenges and leverages their full potential. As Indian organizations continue to embrace these technologies, they must focus on building inclusive, secure, and ethical HR practices to drive sustainable growth.

---

7. AUTOMATION AND ITS IMPACT ON HR AND ORGANIZATIONAL BEHAVIOR (OB)

Automation refers to the use of technology to perform tasks that would commonly require human intervention. In the context of Human Resources (HR) and Organizational Behavior (OB), automation encompasses a variety of tools and technologies designed to streamline administrative tasks, enhance efficiency, and improve decision-making processes. In HR, automation can include recruitment processes (such as applicant tracking systems), performance management systems, payroll automation, and the use of artificial intelligence (AI) for data-driven insights. By automating repetitive and time-consuming tasks, organizations can free up HR professionals to focus on more strategic initiatives, such as talent development and employee engagement.

Author: Harrison, J., & Shipman, J. (2019). The Rise of HR Technology: Automation and its Impact on the Workforce. Human Resource Management Review, 29(2), 197-209.

Automation, driven by advancements in Artificial Intelligence (AI), Machine Learning (ML), and robotics, is reshaping the workplace at an unprecedented pace. In India, where the workforce is vast and diverse, automation is not just a technological shift but a cultural and organizational transformation. This chapter delves into the impact of automation on Human Resources (HR) and Organizational Behavior (OB), exploring how it is redefining roles, processes, and workplace dynamics in Indian organizations.

The advent of automation technologies has brought about transformative changes in the way organizations operate, and Human Resources (HR) is no exception. Automation refers to the use of technology to perform tasks that would otherwise require human intervention. In HR, this involves automating routine administrative tasks, optimizing processes, and enhancing decision-making through AI-driven insights. Similarly, Organizational Behavior (OB)—the study of how individuals and groups behave within an organization—is being redefined by automation tools that influence workplace dynamics, employee engagement, and culture.

In India, where businesses face a rapidly evolving job market and a highly competitive talent pool, automation in HR is gaining significant traction. With a workforce increasingly inclined toward digital tools and agile methodologies, the role of HR has expanded beyond administrative functions to become a more strategic, data-driven partner. The integration of automation into HR and OB has reshaped the way Indian organizations attract talent, manage performance, foster employee engagement, and create a sustainable organizational culture.

The Rise of Automation in the Workplace: Transforming HR and Organizational Behavior in Indian Corporates

Automation has become an essential force reshaping industries worldwide, and its influence is particularly notable in India, where it is rapidly gaining traction across various sectors. The adoption of automation technologies spans industries such as manufacturing, IT, healthcare, and banking, driven by the quest for increased efficiency, cost reduction, and the ability to scale operations more effectively. A 2023 report by McKinsey India highlights that automation could impact up to 60% of jobs in the country, with 25% of tasks potentially being fully automated. This shift is not just about replacing manual labor with machines; it is about enhancing capabilities and improving the overall productivity of the workforce.

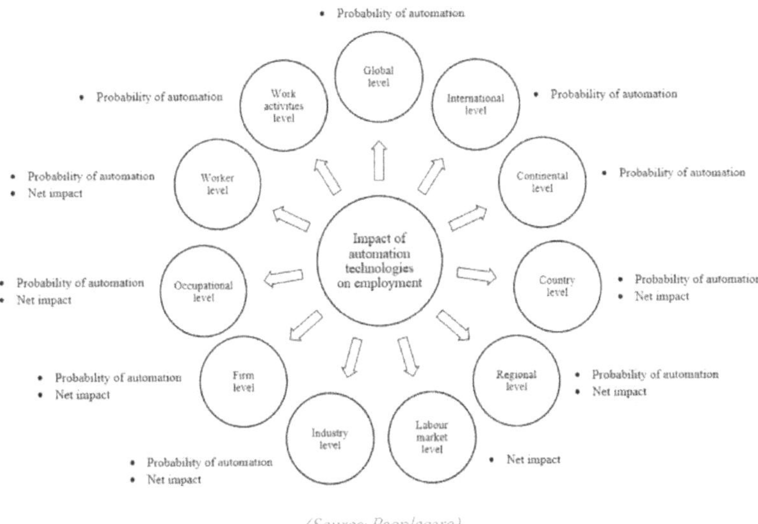

In India, the role of automation is evolving, and it is making its mark in both operational and strategic aspects of businesses. For Human Resources (HR) and Organizational Behavior (OB), automation presents a blend of opportunities and challenges. On one hand, automation streamlines repetitive and time-consuming tasks, thereby enhancing productivity and allowing HR professionals to allocate their time to higher-value activities. For instance, Applicant Tracking Systems (ATS), payroll management software, and AI-driven chatbots are already transforming routine HR functions. ATS simplifies the recruitment process by automating resume screening, reducing the time spent on manual reviews, and ensuring that the most qualified candidates are identified swiftly. Payroll management systems eliminate the need for manual calculation, ensuring accuracy and reducing administrative workload. Similarly, AI-powered chatbots, used for employee queries and basic administrative functions, provide faster responses and an enhanced experience, all while reducing human error.

Automation in HR enables more informed decision-making by providing data-driven insights. HR teams can track employee performance, analyze retention trends, and identify skill gaps using automated systems, which helps in formulating more effective talent management strategies. With the automation of administrative tasks, HR professionals in Indian organizations can shift their focus to areas like strategic workforce planning, leadership development, and employee engagement. For example, organizations like Infosys and Tata Consultancy Services (TCS) are leveraging automation tools to improve their talent acquisition processes and enhance the overall employee experience, allowing HR teams to work more proactively and strategically. By reducing manual errors and ensuring consistency in decision-making, automation in HR functions increases overall operational efficiency.

Granted that, the rise of automation does not come without concerns. A significant challenge lies in the potential for job displacement. As automation takes over routine and administrative tasks, employees may face uncertainties about their roles. Over and above, there is the concern of skill gaps, where workers may not possess the required technical expertise to work alongside these new technologies. To address these issues, HR departments must invest in reskilling and upskilling initiatives to ensure that employees are prepared for the evolving demands of the workforce. In India, organizations are increasingly adopting learning and development (L&D) programs to help employees acquire the skills necessary for emerging roles. Companies like Wipro and HDFC Bank have incorporated digital learning platforms and AI-driven training programs to bridge these skill gaps and ensure their employees are well-equipped for the future.

From an Organizational Behavior perspective, the rise of automation is altering the dynamics of work itself. Automation is changing how employees interact with each other, their managers, and the company as a whole. With the integration of AI and automation tools into day-to-day operations, organizational structures are becoming more dynamic and fluid. Traditional hierarchies are evolving into more agile, decentralized models, where collaboration, innovation, and adaptability are paramount. In this context, employees are increasingly working alongside machines and digital systems, requiring them to develop new skills and mindsets to remain relevant. The role of the manager is also changing—managers are now expected to oversee both human and automated processes, focusing on ensuring that technology is leveraged effectively to enhance team performance rather than replace it.

The work environment in Indian organizations is shifting toward one that is increasingly tech-driven, flexible, and collaborative. Employees now have access to sophisticated digital tools that allow them to work from anywhere, which has significant implications for organizational culture. As automation handles more routine tasks, employees have more time to focus on creative, strategic, and high-level decision-making. This shift is promoting a culture of innovation and adaptability, where employees are encouraged to bring new ideas and solutions to the table. Companies like Flipkart and Mahindra & Mahindra are embracing this change by promoting flexible work models and fostering a culture that encourages experimentation and innovation.

Not to mention, the workplace is becoming increasingly collaborative, as automation tools enable employees to share knowledge, insights, and feedback more efficiently. Cloud-based platforms, AI-driven project management tools, and communication technologies are helping to break down silos within organizations, enabling teams to work together across geographical boundaries. For instance, Indian IT giants like TCS and Infosys have adopted digital collaboration tools that facilitate seamless communication and project management, ensuring that teams remain productive and connected regardless of their physical locations.

Automation in HR: Key Areas of Impact

1. Recruitment and Talent Acquisition

One of the most significant applications of automation in HR is in the recruitment process. Traditional recruitment involves a series of manual steps, from posting job advertisements to screening resumes and conducting interviews. These processes are not only time-consuming but also prone to human bias and error. Automation tools like Applicant Tracking Systems (ATS), AI-powered resume screening, and chatbots have revolutionized this process.

Wipro, one of India's leading IT companies, has implemented an AI-powered recruitment tool that automates resume parsing and shortlisting based on predefined keywords, skills, and experience. This tool helps reduce the time HR professionals spend on initial screening and ensures that only the most suitable candidates are shortlisted. Similarly, tools like *HireVue* and *Talview* are helping organizations in India conduct virtual interviews and assess candidate responses through AI-driven video analytics, providing HR teams with deeper insights into candidate suitability.

A 2022 *People Matters* survey found that 67% of Indian organizations that adopted automation in recruitment experienced a reduction of up to 30% in the time spent on the hiring process, with 80% of HR professionals reporting improved quality in candidate selection.

2. Employee Onboarding

Employee onboarding is another area where automation has made a significant impact. The onboarding process usually involves a lot of paperwork, training sessions, and manual data entry, all of which are time-consuming for both HR professionals and new hires. Automation tools like *WorkBright* and *BambooHR* help streamline onboarding by automating document management, benefits enrollment, and training schedules.

For example, *Infosys* has integrated an automated onboarding system that walks new employees through each step of the process, from document submission to training. This system not only reduces administrative work but also creates a more personalized and engaging experience for the new hires, ensuring that they feel welcomed and informed.

A 2023 study by *LinkedIn Talent Solutions* found that 80% of Indian companies that implemented automated onboarding systems reported higher new-hire engagement and reduced turnover rates, with some organizations experiencing a 40% reduction in the time required to complete the onboarding process.

3. Performance Management and Employee Engagement

Performance management is an ongoing process that requires continuous monitoring, feedback, and evaluation. Generally, performance reviews have been based on subjective assessments and often occurred on an annual basis. With the rise of automation, HR departments in India are moving toward more frequent, data-driven, and objective performance evaluations.

AI-powered performance management systems, like those used by *Tata Consultancy Services (TCS)* and *Larsen &*

Toubro, gather data on employee performance in real-time, automatically generating reports that highlight strengths, areas for improvement, and overall progress toward organizational goals. This automated feedback mechanism enables HR to provide timely, actionable insights to employees, fostering continuous development and improvement.

Collocations, automated employee engagement tools, such as *Officevibe* and *TINYpulse*, use real-time surveys and sentiment analysis to measure employee satisfaction and engagement. These tools help HR teams identify issues such as burnout, lack of recognition, or communication gaps, allowing them to address these concerns proactively.

In a 2023 survey by *McKinsey*, 72% of Indian organizations using automated performance management systems reported increased employee productivity and engagement. These tools enabled managers to focus on coaching and development, rather than spending time on administrative tasks.

4. Payroll and Benefits Administration

Payroll processing is one of the most repetitive and error-prone tasks in HR. Automating payroll systems not only ensures that employees are paid accurately and on time but also minimizes administrative overheads. Indian companies like *HCL Technologies* and *Wipro* have implemented automated payroll solutions that integrate with other HR systems to ensure seamless processing of salaries, bonuses, and benefits.

For that reason, automation in benefits administration is helping employees manage their benefits, such as health insurance, retirement plans, and paid time off, more efficiently. Automated platforms allow employees to view and modify their benefits in real-time, improving transparency and satisfaction.

A report by *PwC India* in 2023 revealed that automation in payroll processing led to a 20-25% reduction in operational costs for organizations, with an associated 30% reduction in payroll-related errors.

Automation's Impact on Organizational Behavior (OB)

1. Changing Employee Dynamics and Job Roles

Automation has a significant impact on organizational behavior by altering the way employees interact with their work and colleagues. As routine tasks are automated, employees are freed up to focus on more strategic and creative tasks, which can lead to increased job satisfaction and motivation. This shift in responsibilities encourages employees to develop new skills, leading to a more agile and adaptable workforce.

Nevertheless, automation can also lead to job displacement, particularly for roles that involve repetitive tasks. This creates a need for organizations to upskill and reskill their employees to prepare them for more advanced, technology-driven roles. Indian organizations such as *Infosys* and *Tech Mahindra* are investing heavily in reskilling programs to help employees transition into roles that require higher-order thinking and technological expertise.

According to a 2023 *World Economic Forum* report, 45% of Indian workers are expected to undergo reskilling or upskilling in the next five years to adapt to the growing impact of automation in the workplace.

2. Enhancing Organizational Culture and Communication

Automation tools also play a role in improving communication and collaboration across organizational levels. By automating administrative tasks, HR professionals and managers can devote more time to fostering an open, transparent, and inclusive workplace culture. Tools like *Slack* and *Microsoft Teams*, combined with automated workflows, are enabling employees to collaborate seamlessly, regardless of their physical location.

Accordingly, automation can help bridge gaps in communication, especially in remote and hybrid work environments. Automated notifications, reminders, and updates ensure that employees remain engaged and informed, reducing the chances of miscommunication.

3. Promoting Work-Life Balance

Automation can also promote work-life balance by reducing employee burnout and stress. By automating repetitive tasks, employees can focus on more fulfilling and intellectually stimulating work, leading to higher job satisfaction and a better work-life balance. Withal, automated systems for time-off requests, flexible work scheduling, and workload management can contribute to a healthier work environment.

A 2023 study by *Forbes India* found that 60% of employees working in organizations that implemented automation reported an improved work-life balance, with 50% also citing higher levels of job satisfaction.

Case Studies: Automation in Indian Organizations

Several Indian organizations have successfully integrated automation into their HR and OB practices:

Infosys: The IT giant has implemented an AI-driven recruitment platform that has reduced hiring time by 30% and improved the quality of hires.

HDFC Bank: The bank uses automated performance management systems to track employee performance and provide real-time feedback, resulting in a 20% improvement in productivity.

Tata Steel: The company has launched a "Future Ready" program to help employees transition to automated roles, improving employee confidence and retention.

Automation is rapidly transforming HR and Organizational Behavior practices in Indian organizations. By automating routine tasks, organizations can improve efficiency, reduce errors, and enhance employee engagement. Just the same, the impact of automation extends beyond HR functions—it also reshapes organizational culture, job roles, and employee dynamics. As Indian organizations continue to adopt automation, HR departments must play a strategic role in ensuring a smooth transition and addressing the challenges posed by this technological shift. With the right approach, automation can empower HR professionals and employees to thrive in an increasingly digital and dynamic workplace.

8: THE ROLE OF OKRS AND KPIS IN DRIVING PERFORMANCE AND STRATEGY IN INDIAN ORGANIZATIONS

OKRs are a goal-setting framework used by organizations to set clear and measurable objectives, along with the key results that indicate progress toward achieving these objectives. OKRs help align individual, team, and organizational goals, ensuring that everyone is working towards the same overarching vision. Objectives are qualitative, while key results are quantitative metrics that track performance. The framework encourages transparency, accountability, and continuous progress tracking, often used in leading tech companies like Google.

KPIs, on the other hand, are specific, measurable metrics that an organization uses to gauge its performance in different areas. While OKRs are broader in scope and focus on strategic goals, KPIs are typically narrower, assessing operational success, productivity, and the achievement of specific performance standards. Both OKRs and KPIs are essential tools for performance management, but OKRs are generally more aligned with long-term strategic goals, whereas KPIs monitor day-to-day operations and success.

Author: *Doerr, J. (2018). Measure What Matters: OKRs: The Simple Idea that Drives 10x Growth. Portfolio Penguin.*

In the fast-paced and competitive business environment of India, organizations are constantly seeking ways to enhance performance, align teams, and achieve strategic goals. Two of the most widely adopted frameworks for achieving these objectives are Objectives and Key Results (OKRs) and Key Performance Indicators (KPIs). While OKRs focus on setting ambitious goals and measuring outcomes, KPIs provide a quantitative measure of performance against specific targets. Together, these frameworks enable organizations to drive accountability, foster innovation, and achieve sustainable growth. This chapter explores the role of OKRs and KPIs in Indian organizations, their implementation challenges, and best practices for success.

While OKRs focus on setting ambitious goals with measurable outcomes, KPIs are the metrics that help track performance against predefined targets. Together, these two frameworks enable businesses to align their strategic vision with day-to-day operations, improve efficiency, and drive growth.

This chapter will explore the roles of OKRs and KPIs in Indian organizations, emphasizing their impact on performance, alignment, and organizational success. Through case studies and recent trends, we will see how Indian companies are integrating these tools into their performance management systems to achieve remarkable results.

The Growing Adoption of OKRs and KPIs in India: Enhancing Performance and Alignment in Indian Organizations

In recent years, the adoption of performance management frameworks such as OKRs (Objectives and Key Results) and KPIs (Key Performance Indicators) has significantly grown across Indian organizations, becoming essential tools for driving alignment, performance, and organizational success. According to a 2023 survey by Deloitte India, approximately 65% of Indian companies have adopted the OKR framework, while 80% use KPIs to measure and track performance. This shift reflects the growing need for organizations in India to stay competitive, innovate continuously, and manage an increasingly dynamic workforce.

The increasing adoption of OKRs and KPIs in Indian corporates can be attributed to the rapid changes in the business environment, especially in industries that demand high levels of agility and innovation. Sectors like IT, e-commerce, and startups are particularly embracing these frameworks due to their ability to foster alignment across teams, ensure measurable progress, and track key outcomes. With the need for organizations to adapt quickly to market demands, the use of OKRs and KPIs offers a structured approach to set clear goals and monitor progress, helping organizations stay focused on the desired results.

In India, several organizations have leveraged OKRs and KPIs to enhance their operational efficiency and achieve business objectives. For example, Flipkart, one of the country's largest e-commerce giants, has implemented the OKR framework with great success. The company has used OKRs to align its diverse teams and ensure that all departments are working toward common organizational goals. By setting specific, measurable objectives such as "Increase customer retention by 20%" and tracking key results like "Reduce delivery time by 15%," Flipkart has been able to focus its efforts on areas that directly impact customer satisfaction and operational performance. This alignment has been instrumental in Flipkart's ability to maintain its competitive edge and drive growth in the rapidly evolving e-commerce sector.

The use of OKRs and KPIs has also been widely adopted by leading Indian IT companies, such as Infosys and TCS. These organizations have integrated the frameworks into their performance management systems to ensure that their teams are consistently working toward strategic priorities. By focusing on measurable results, these companies have been able to drive greater efficiency and performance across their projects, from client delivery to employee engagement.

KPIs, which have been in use for a longer time, continue to be a fundamental part of performance measurement in Indian organizations. They provide organizations with concrete metrics to assess individual, team, and organizational performance. KPIs are especially prevalent in sectors like manufacturing, banking, and telecommunications, where operational efficiency and meeting service-level expectations are key priorities. For example, in the banking sector, companies like HDFC Bank and ICICI Bank use KPIs to monitor financial metrics, customer satisfaction, and operational processes, enabling them to deliver services more efficiently and maintain high levels of performance.

The adoption of OKRs and KPIs is not limited to large corporations. Indian startups, with their focus on scalability, innovation, and speed, have also been quick to embrace these performance frameworks. Startups, like Zomato and Swiggy, use OKRs to align their teams with ambitious growth goals. These organizations benefit from the clarity and transparency provided by the OKR system, enabling them to rapidly pivot and adjust strategies in a highly competitive market. Over and above, by tracking KPIs related to customer acquisition, engagement, and retention, these startups ensure that their growth is sustainable and that they remain focused on driving meaningful outcomes.

Differences	OKR's	KPI's
PURPOSE	Focus & Alignment	Evaluating Activities
SCOPE	Broad Vision	Narrow Vision
DURATION	Short term goal	Long-term goal
BUILDABLE	No	No
FLEXIBLE	Yes	Yes

The growth of OKRs and KPIs in India is not just a passing trend, but part of a broader cultural shift toward data-driven decision-making and accountability within organizations. Indian companies, whether large or small, are increasingly recognizing the importance of aligning their employees' individual efforts with organizational goals. This focus on measurable outcomes has led to a more results-oriented corporate culture, where success is determined not just by effort but by the ability to achieve and surpass specific objectives.

To boot, the use of OKRs and KPIs is enhancing transparency within organizations. Employees have a clear understanding of what is expected of them, and they can track their progress toward achieving organizational objectives. This transparency fosters a sense of ownership and accountability, leading to greater employee engagement and motivation. As a result, HR professionals in Indian organizations are using OKRs and KPIs as tools for performance management and employee development. By incorporating these frameworks into annual reviews, feedback sessions, and career progression discussions, HR departments ensure that employees are not only meeting performance standards but are also aligned with the strategic direction of the company.

As Indian organizations continue to evolve and face increasing competition in the global marketplace, the adoption of OKRs and KPIs will play a pivotal role in shaping the future of performance management. The ability to measure progress, set clear goals, and track results will be critical for driving organizational growth, fostering a high-performance culture, and maintaining employee alignment. As more Indian companies embrace these frameworks, the future of work in India will be characterized by a greater focus on goal clarity, measurable outcomes, and continuous performance improvement.

Understanding OKRs and KPIs

1. OKRs: A Framework for Goal Setting and Alignment

OKRs were introduced by Andy Grove at Intel in the 1970s and later popularized by John Doerr, a venture capitalist who introduced the concept to companies like Google. The OKR framework is designed to set ambitious, high-level goals (Objectives) and then break them down into measurable results (Key Results). OKRs are typically set quarterly or annually, and they are intended to drive focus, transparency, and accountability within an organization.

The key elements of OKRs are:

- **Objectives**: Clear, qualitative goals that provide direction and inspiration.

- **Key Results**: Quantifiable outcomes that measure progress toward achieving the objectives.

- **Alignment**: OKRs align individual and team goals with the overall company strategy, ensuring that everyone is working toward the same outcomes.

2. KPIs: Measuring Progress and Performance

KPIs, on the other hand, are the quantifiable metrics used to gauge performance in specific areas. KPIs are often tied to operational processes, such as revenue growth, customer acquisition, or employee productivity. Unlike OKRs, which are more about goal setting, KPIs are primarily about tracking ongoing performance and ensuring that operations stay on course to meet the strategic objectives.

The key elements of KPIs are:

- **Actionability**: KPIs should reflect key areas that are important for business success and provide insights into performance.

- **Specificity**: KPIs are typically narrower in scope than OKRs and are often tied to particular departments or processes.

- **Measurability**: KPIs are quantifiable and used for continuous monitoring, such as tracking sales, customer satisfaction scores, or operational efficiency.

The Role of OKRs and KPIs in Indian Organizations

Indian organizations are increasingly adopting OKRs and KPIs to streamline their performance management processes, particularly as the business landscape becomes more competitive and fast-paced. According to a 2022 survey by *People Matters*, 57% of Indian organizations reported that they had started using OKRs as part of their strategic planning and performance management systems.

Below, we discuss how OKRs and KPIs are being used in Indian organizations to drive growth, improve efficiency, and align teams.

1. Strategic Alignment with OKRs

In India, where businesses operate in diverse sectors ranging from technology to manufacturing, aligning teams with a unified organizational vision is often challenging. OKRs provide a clear framework to ensure that every department and individual is working towards the same strategic goals.

For example, *Infosys*, one of India's leading IT firms, uses OKRs at every level of the organization, from the CEO to individual contributors. By setting specific, measurable, and time-bound objectives, Infosys ensures that its teams remain aligned with the broader organizational mission. The company uses OKRs to focus on key goals like customer satisfaction, innovation, and operational efficiency, while individual performance metrics (KPIs) track how well employees are executing their tasks to meet those objectives.

Similarly, *Flipkart*, a major player in India's e-commerce space, implemented OKRs in 2019 to align its various teams, including engineering, marketing, and customer service, with the company's growth targets. By setting clear OKRs, Flipkart ensures that its teams are not just working hard but working in alignment with the company's overarching goals, resulting in improved collaboration and better outcomes.

2. Driving Employee Engagement with OKRs

Employee engagement is a significant concern for many Indian organizations, where traditional hierarchical structures and management practices often hinder open communication and alignment. OKRs help to create a culture of transparency and accountability, giving employees a sense of ownership over their work. When employees can clearly see how their individual goals contribute to the company's success, they are more likely to stay motivated and engaged.

In a study by *Gallup India* (2021), organizations that integrated OKRs into their performance management system reported a 32% higher employee engagement rate compared to companies that did not use OKRs. Employees who understand the direct impact of their work are more likely to be proactive, contributing to higher productivity and retention.

Tata Consultancy Services (TCS), one of India's largest IT services companies, uses OKRs to ensure that employees understand their roles in driving business outcomes. TCS has integrated OKRs with their learning and development initiatives, ensuring that employees are continuously learning and growing in alignment with company objectives. This not only boosts engagement but also fosters a culture of continuous improvement.

3. Measuring Performance with KPIs

While OKRs set the stage for goal alignment, KPIs provide the necessary tools for measuring progress and performance. KPIs are essential for tracking the effectiveness of operations, identifying areas for improvement, and ensuring that teams are on track to meet their OKRs.

In India, many companies have integrated KPIs with their day-to-day operations to ensure that they are delivering measurable results. For instance, *Hindustan Unilever Limited (HUL)* uses KPIs to monitor key operational metrics such as market share, customer satisfaction, and product quality. These KPIs help HUL's leadership team make data-driven decisions and quickly adapt to changing market conditions.

Yet, Indian startups are increasingly using KPIs to gauge their success in areas such as customer acquisition, sales growth, and customer retention. A case in point is *Zomato*, a leading food delivery platform, which uses KPIs to monitor key aspects of its business, such as the average order value, delivery time, and customer feedback. These KPIs are closely tied to the company's OKRs, ensuring that Zomato is consistently working towards its growth and customer satisfaction objectives.

4. Improving Business Outcomes

Both OKRs and KPIs contribute to better business outcomes by providing clarity and focus. OKRs set the direction for where the company wants to go, while KPIs help track progress and ensure that the organization stays on course. Together, these frameworks provide a holistic approach to performance management, driving efficiency and accountability at every level.

For example, *Mahindra & Mahindra*, one of India's leading industrial conglomerates, uses both OKRs and KPIs to ensure its growth in the highly competitive automotive sector. The company sets ambitious OKRs for market expansion, innovation, and customer satisfaction. These are complemented by KPIs that monitor key operational areas such as production efficiency, sales conversion rates, and after-sales service.

By using both frameworks, Mahindra is able to ensure that its teams are aligned with the company's strategic objectives while also tracking performance through measurable metrics.

Best Practices for Implementing OKRs and KPIs

To overcome these challenges and maximize the benefits of OKRs and KPIs, Indian organizations can adopt the following best practices:

1. **Start Small and Scale Gradually:** Begin with a pilot project in one department or team before rolling out OKRs and KPIs across the organization. This allows for experimentation and learning.

2. **Ensure Leadership Buy-In:** Leadership support is critical for the successful implementation of OKRs and KPIs. Leaders must model the desired behaviors and actively participate in the process.

3. **Provide Training and Resources:** Equip employees and managers with the knowledge and tools they need to set effective OKRs and KPIs. Regular training sessions and workshops can help build capability.

4. **Foster a Culture of Collaboration:** Encourage cross-functional collaboration and communication to ensure alignment and shared ownership of goals.

5. **Regularly Review and Adjust:** OKRs and KPIs should be reviewed regularly to track progress, identify gaps, and make necessary adjustments. Quarterly reviews are a common practice in organizations using OKRs.

Challenges of Implementing OKRs and KPIs

With many benefits of OKRs and KPIs, Indian organizations face several challenges when implementing these frameworks:

Resistance to Change: Introducing OKRs and KPIs can face resistance from employees, particularly in organizations with traditional, hierarchical cultures. There may be concerns about transparency, accountability, and the perceived pressure of meeting ambitious goals.

Overcomplication of Metrics: Organizations must be cautious not to overwhelm employees with too many KPIs. Overcomplicating the performance measurement process can lead to confusion and disengagement. Focusing too much on KPIs can lead to a narrow focus on short-term results at the expense of long-term goals. For example, a sales team might prioritize meeting monthly revenue targets (a KPI) over building customer relationships, which could harm long-term growth.

Alignment Issues: Ensuring that OKRs and KPIs are aligned across all levels of the organization can be a challenge, particularly in large, complex organizations. Without proper communication and coordination, the risk of misalignment is high.

Lack of Follow-Through: Setting OKRs and KPIs is only part of the equation. Organizations must ensure that they are regularly tracking progress, providing feedback, and making adjustments as needed to stay on course. Many organizations struggle to define clear objectives and key results, leading to confusion and misalignment. A 2023 survey by KPMG India found that 40% of employees in organizations using OKRs were unclear about how their work contributed to the overall objectives.

Case Studies: OKRs and KPIs in Indian Organizations

Byju's: The edtech giant uses OKRs to drive innovation and growth. For example, one of its objectives is "Enhance user engagement," with key results like "Increase daily active users by 15%" and "Improve course completion rates by 10%."

Mahindra & Mahindra: The automotive leader uses KPIs to measure performance across its manufacturing and sales teams. Key metrics include production efficiency, sales growth, and customer satisfaction.

Ola: The ride-hailing platform uses OKRs to align its teams and achieve strategic goals. One of its objectives is "Expand into new markets," with key results like "Launch operations in 5 new cities" and "Achieve 10,000 rides per day in new markets."

OKRs and KPIs are powerful tools that help organizations drive performance, align teams, and measure success. In Indian organizations, these frameworks are becoming increasingly important as businesses seek to navigate the complexities of a rapidly changing market. Through the use of OKRs, organizations can set clear, ambitious goals that align their workforce with the company's vision. KPIs, on the other hand, allow businesses to track progress and ensure that they are on the right path.

9. UPSKILLING AND RESKILLING THE WORKFORCE: PREPARING INDIA FOR THE FUTURE OF WORK

In an era defined by rapid technological advancements, economic shifts, and evolving job roles, the need for upskilling and reskilling the workforce has never been more critical. For India, a country with a young and dynamic population, this challenge is both an opportunity and a necessity. With over 65% of its population under the age of 35, India has the potential to become a global talent hub. Though, realizing this potential requires a concerted effort to equip the workforce with the skills needed to thrive in the future of work.

In a world defined by rapid technological advancements, shifting market dynamics, and evolving business models, the demand for a highly adaptable and capable workforce has never been greater. Organizations worldwide, including those in India, are facing the challenge of equipping their employees with the right skills to remain competitive. In this context, upskilling and reskilling have become crucial strategies to ensure that employees can thrive in the face of change.

- **Upskilling** refers to enhancing the existing skills of employees to improve their performance and productivity.

- **Reskilling** involves training employees to take on new roles or responsibilities, especially in areas that require entirely different skills.

Both upskilling and reskilling are key strategies for organizations to stay competitive in the face of changing technological, economic, and industry conditions, while also ensuring employees' career growth and job satisfaction.

Author: Bersin, J. (2018). The Employee Experience: How to Attract Talent, Develop Talent, and Keep Talent. Deloitte Review, 22.

As the nature of work continues to evolve, the need for continuous learning and development has become more critical. Indian organizations are increasingly prioritizing upskilling and reskilling initiatives to stay competitive, meet the demands of the digital economy, and empower their workforce to take on future challenges.

This chapter delves into the significance of upskilling and reskilling in Indian organizations, examining the benefits, challenges, and best practices, supported by recent case studies and industry trends.

The Imperative for Upskilling and Reskilling: Navigating the Changing Landscape of Work in India

The Fourth Industrial Revolution, which is driven by advancements in automation, artificial intelligence (AI), and digital transformation, is radically changing industries and the nature of job roles across the globe. As technological innovations continue to evolve, the demand for new skills and capabilities is growing, making it imperative for workers to continuously upskill and reskill to stay relevant in the ever-changing job market. According to a 2023 report by the World Economic Forum (WEF), 50% of all employees globally will need reskilling by 2025, and in India, this need is even more urgent. A NASSCOM study suggests that around 60% of India's workforce will require upskilling or reskilling to remain relevant in the face of rapid technological change.

Author's Creation

The need for upskilling and reskilling has been further accelerated by the COVID-19 pandemic, which forced organizations to adopt remote work, embrace digital tools, and rethink their business models. This sudden and massive shift highlighted the importance of adaptability, digital literacy, and the ability to thrive in virtual environments. For many Indian organizations, the pandemic underscored the necessity of upskilling initiatives that could enable their employees to adapt to new tools, platforms, and processes in a timely manner.

A 2023 LinkedIn survey found that 75% of Indian professionals believe their current skills will become obsolete within the next five years, highlighting the urgency of upskilling and reskilling initiatives. This sense of urgency is not just a reaction to the pandemic but also a response to the increasing automation of tasks and the growing demand for new competencies, such as AI, machine learning, data analytics, and digital marketing. As organizations in India integrate these technologies into their operations, employees must possess the right set of skills to work alongside intelligent systems and contribute to innovative business strategies.

For HR and OB professionals in India, the need for upskilling and reskilling presents both a challenge and an opportunity. On the one hand, there is the daunting task of ensuring that employees acquire the skills needed to meet the demands of a digitalized workplace. On the other hand, it offers the opportunity to create a culture of continuous learning and development that fosters innovation, resilience, and employee satisfaction. Indian organizations that invest in employee development are not only preparing their workforce for the future but also strengthening their competitive advantage in a rapidly changing market.

Indian companies are responding to this imperative by designing and implementing various upskilling and reskilling programs tailored to different employee needs. For instance, major IT and tech firms such as TCS, Infosys, and Wipro have launched training programs focused on emerging technologies like cloud computing, cybersecurity, and AI. These programs often include online courses, workshops, mentorship, and even partnerships with educational institutions to ensure that employees stay up-to-date with industry trends and advancements. So, companies are increasingly adopting personalized learning paths that allow employees to pursue skills relevant to their specific roles or future career aspirations.

Too, the shift to remote work and the rise of digital learning platforms have made upskilling and reskilling more accessible to Indian employees. Organizations are leveraging platforms like LinkedIn Learning, Coursera, and Udemy to provide employees with flexible, on-demand courses that they can complete at their own pace. These digital platforms offer employees the opportunity to enhance their knowledge in areas such as project management, digital marketing, and leadership, without having to leave their work environment.

The growing importance of soft skills, such as emotional intelligence, adaptability, and collaboration, in the digital age cannot be overlooked. Indian organizations are increasingly recognizing that while technical skills are crucial, the ability to work effectively with others, manage change, and think critically are just as important. Many companies are therefore incorporating soft skills training into their reskilling initiatives to ensure their workforce can thrive in increasingly collaborative and fast-paced work environments.

A second point to consider to these formal training programs, Indian organizations are also encouraging a culture of learning through internal knowledge-sharing initiatives. Many companies have set up platforms for employees to share expertise, collaborate on projects, and learn from one another. This collaborative learning environment fosters innovation and enables employees to broaden their skillsets beyond their immediate job functions.

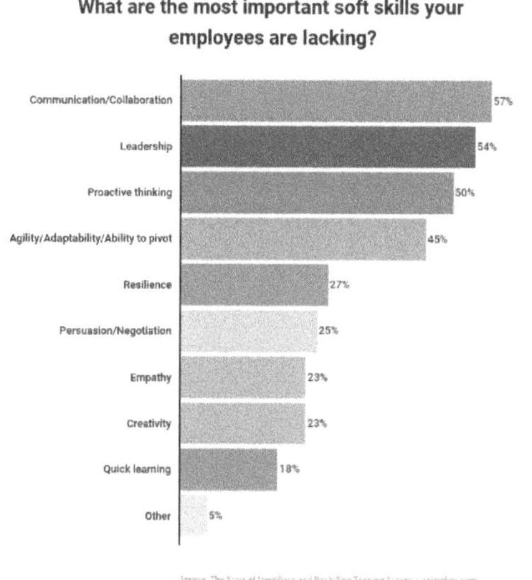

One of the critical areas in which Indian organizations are focusing their upskilling efforts is leadership development. With the pace of change in the business world, there is a growing need for leaders who can navigate complex challenges, lead through uncertainty, and inspire their teams to embrace new technologies. Companies such as Reliance Industries, Tata Group, and Mahindra & Mahindra are investing heavily in leadership training programs that prepare their future leaders to take on strategic roles in a digital-first economy.

The importance of upskilling and reskilling is not only being recognized by large corporations but also by startups and small and medium-sized enterprises (SMEs) in India. These organizations, which are often at the forefront of innovation, understand that a skilled workforce is essential to their growth and sustainability. As a result, they are increasingly adopting flexible training programs that provide their employees with the skills they need to scale their operations and meet changing customer demands.

For HR and OB professionals, it is crucial to not only design and implement effective upskilling and reskilling programs but also to create a culture that values continuous learning. This includes offering career development opportunities, recognizing employees who demonstrate a commitment to learning, and fostering an environment where employees feel supported in their growth. HR professionals must work closely with business leaders to ensure that learning initiatives are aligned with organizational goals and that employees are given the resources they need to succeed.

The Growing Importance of Upskilling and Reskilling

1. Adapting to Technological Changes

The pace of technological innovation has accelerated, especially with the rise of artificial intelligence (AI), machine learning (ML), automation, and data analytics. In India, organizations across various sectors are adopting these technologies to enhance operational efficiency, improve customer experiences, and drive innovation.

Still, the implementation of these technologies often necessitates the development of new skills. Employees need to adapt to new tools, software, and methodologies. This is where upskilling and reskilling come into play. By investing in these initiatives, organizations ensure that their employees are equipped to work alongside advanced technologies, rather than being displaced by them.

For example, *Infosys*, one of India's largest IT services companies, has made significant investments in reskilling its workforce to handle new-age technologies such as cloud computing, AI, and blockchain. Through its "InStep" program, Infosys provides its employees with opportunities to learn new skills, ensuring they are prepared for the challenges and opportunities brought about by digital transformation.

2. Meeting Industry Demands and Skills Gap

The skills gap in India is a significant concern for employers. Many industries are grappling with a shortage of skilled talent, particularly in fields like data science, cybersecurity, and digital marketing. According to a report by *NASSCOM* (2022), around 50% of employers in India are struggling to find candidates with the right skills for emerging roles.

Upskilling and reskilling programs help bridge this gap by equipping employees with the specific skills needed to fill high-demand roles. This not only addresses the talent shortage but also enhances employee satisfaction and retention by offering career development opportunities.

Organizations such as *Tata Consultancy Services (TCS)* have invested heavily in training their employees through digital platforms like TCS iON, which provides learning content in areas such as digital literacy, business analytics, and AI. TCS's emphasis on continuous learning enables its workforce to stay ahead of industry trends and position the company as a leader in the competitive IT services sector.

3. Supporting Career Growth and Employee Retention

Employee retention is an ongoing challenge in many organizations. A key factor influencing an employee's decision to stay with a company is the opportunity for growth and development. When employees are offered the chance to upskill or reskill, it fosters a sense of career progression and loyalty.

For instance, *Hindustan Unilever Limited (HUL)* has established various learning and development programs aimed at enhancing employees' skills, such as leadership training, digital literacy courses, and technical expertise development. HUL's commitment to employee growth is a major reason why it is consistently ranked as one of the top companies to work for in India.

Upskilling programs also help employees stay motivated and engaged, as they see tangible returns in terms of career advancement and new opportunities. By providing clear pathways for growth, organizations can not only reduce turnover but also attract top talent in a competitive job market.

Key Trends in Upskilling and Reskilling in Indian Organizations

1. The Shift Toward Digital Learning Platforms

As the demand for continuous learning grows, many Indian organizations are turning to digital learning platforms to deliver upskilling and reskilling programs. These platforms offer flexibility, allowing employees to learn at their own pace and convenience. The rise of Massive Open Online Courses (MOOCs), e-learning modules, and virtual training sessions has revolutionized how organizations approach workforce development.

Platforms like *Coursera*, *Udemy*, and *LinkedIn Learning* are popular choices in Indian organizations for providing employees with access to a wide range of courses in areas such as programming, digital marketing, and data analytics. These platforms are often integrated into companies' internal learning management systems, allowing employees to track their progress and access relevant learning materials.

For example, *Wipro* offers its employees access to a wide range of e-learning resources through its "Wipro Academy of Software Excellence" (WASE). This initiative is part of the company's strategy to ensure that employees are constantly developing new skills that are aligned with the company's technological advancements.

2. Focus on Soft Skills and Leadership Development

While technical skills are important, soft skills are equally critical in today's workforce. Skills such as communication, problem-solving, teamwork, and leadership are increasingly sought after by Indian employers. As companies evolve into more dynamic and collaborative environments, soft skills are becoming a key differentiator in employee performance.

Companies like *Accenture* India have recognized the need to focus on leadership development and soft skills training. Accenture's "Leadership Essentials" program, which includes modules on emotional intelligence, conflict resolution, and communication, has proven to be an effective way of preparing employees for leadership roles. By investing in soft skills, Indian organizations can create a more engaged, productive, and effective workforce.

3. Government and Industry Initiatives

The Indian government, in collaboration with private sector companies, has launched various initiatives to promote upskilling and reskilling in the country. The *Skill India* initiative, launched by the Indian government in 2015, aims to train over 400 million people in various skills by 2022. This initiative focuses on providing industry-specific training and creating job-ready talent to meet the demands of the growing economy.

Side by side, industry bodies like *NASSCOM* have launched initiatives to address the skills gap in the IT sector. NASSCOM's "FutureSkills" platform offers employees in the tech industry the opportunity to upskill in areas such as artificial intelligence, data analytics, and cybersecurity. By collaborating with industry bodies, Indian organizations can tap into a wider pool of resources and training programs to support their workforce development efforts.

Challenges in Upskilling and Reskilling

With the clear benefits, Indian organizations face several challenges in implementing upskilling and reskilling initiatives:

Lack of Awareness and Motivation: Many employees are unaware of the need for upskilling or lack the motivation to pursue it. A 2023 survey by PwC India found that 40% of Indian workers are reluctant to engage in reskilling programs due to time constraints or a lack of interest.

Resource Constraints: Small and medium-sized enterprises (SMEs) often lack the resources to invest in comprehensive training programs. According to a 2023 report by the Confederation of Indian Industry (CII), 60% of SMEs in India struggle to allocate budgets for upskilling initiatives.

Rapidly Changing Skill Requirements: The pace of technological change makes it difficult for organizations to identify and prioritize the skills needed for the future. A 2023 study by McKinsey India highlighted that 50% of Indian companies find it challenging to keep their upskilling programs aligned with industry trends.

Measuring ROI: Organizations often struggle to measure the return on investment (ROI) of upskilling and reskilling programs, making it difficult to justify continued investment.

Strategies for Effective Upskilling and Reskilling

To overcome these challenges and build a future-ready workforce, Indian organizations are adopting innovative strategies:

Leveraging Technology: Digital platforms and e-learning tools are making upskilling more accessible and cost-effective. Companies like TCS and Wipro have developed online learning platforms that offer personalized training programs. For example, TCS's "Digital Learning Zone" provides employees with access to over 200,000 courses on emerging technologies.

Collaborating with Educational Institutions: Partnerships with universities and training institutes help organizations align their upskilling programs with industry needs. For instance, HCL Technologies has partnered with the Indian Institutes of Technology (IITs) to offer specialized courses in AI and machine learning.

Focusing on Soft Skills: In withal to technical skills, organizations are emphasizing the importance of soft skills like communication, critical thinking, and emotional intelligence. A 2023 report by LinkedIn found that 85% of Indian employers consider soft skills as important as technical skills for career success.

Government Initiatives: The Indian government has launched several initiatives to promote upskilling, such as the Skill India Mission and the National Skill Development Corporation (NSDC). These programs provide funding, training, and certification opportunities for both employees and employers.

Creating a Culture of Continuous Learning: Organizations are fostering a culture of lifelong learning by encouraging employees to take ownership of their development. For example, Mahindra & Mahindra has introduced a "Learn and

Earn" program that rewards employees for completing upskilling courses.

Case Studies: Upskilling and Reskilling in Indian Organizations

Infosys: The IT giant's "Reskill and Restart" program has trained thousands of employees in emerging technologies, enabling them to transition to new roles and projects.

Tata Steel: The company's "Project Akanksha" focuses on upskilling employees in digital tools and technologies, helping them adapt to the changing demands of the steel industry.

Amazon India: The e-commerce leader has launched the "Amazon Technical Academy" to train employees in software development, bridging the skills gap in the tech sector.

As Indian organizations continue to navigate a complex and competitive business environment, upskilling and reskilling will play a pivotal role in their success. By investing in the development of their workforce, organizations can foster innovation, improve productivity, and ensure long-term growth.

From enabling employees to embrace new technologies to fostering leadership skills and soft skills, upskilling and reskilling are critical in shaping the future of work. While challenges exist, organizations that implement thoughtful, comprehensive training programs stand to gain not only from a more capable workforce but also from increased employee satisfaction, retention, and overall business success.

The commitment to upskilling and reskilling reflects a forward-thinking approach that will be crucial for Indian organizations as they prepare to thrive in the digital age.

10: EQUITY AND TRANSPARENCY IN PAY STRUCTURES: BUILDING TRUST AND FAIRNESS IN INDIAN ORGANIZATIONS

Pay equity and transparency have emerged as critical issues in the modern workplace, particularly in India, where diversity, inclusion, and employee satisfaction are increasingly prioritized. A fair and transparent pay structure not only fosters trust and loyalty among employees but also enhances organizational reputation and competitiveness. For all that, achieving pay equity and transparency is a complex challenge, especially in a country as diverse as India, where disparities in gender, region, and industry often lead to unequal compensation.

In today's competitive business environment, equity and transparency in pay structures are not just legal obligations but essential pillars of trust, employee satisfaction, and organizational success. Employees increasingly expect fairness in compensation, with an emphasis on both internal and external equity. Internal equity refers to fairness in pay among employees within an organization, while external equity ensures that compensation is competitive relative to the industry standards and regional markets.

In India, a diverse country with a rapidly evolving corporate landscape, the conversation around pay equity and transparency has gained significant momentum. With a young, highly educated workforce, the expectations for fair compensation are higher than ever before. Companies are under increasing pressure to adopt transparent and equitable pay structures to attract and retain talent, build trust, and foster a culture of inclusivity.

The Importance of Equity and Transparency in Pay Structures

1. Attracting and Retaining Talent

In an increasingly competitive job market, organizations that offer fair and transparent pay structures are more likely to attract top talent. Pay equity helps potential employees feel that they are entering a workplace where merit, skill, and experience are rewarded fairly. Transparency in pay structures reassures candidates that salaries are not influenced by biases, favoritism, or hidden discrepancies.

For instance, *Tata Consultancy Services (TCS)*, one of India's largest IT service providers, has implemented clear and well-structured pay scales, ensuring that employees know how their compensation compares to industry standards. This transparency helps TCS retain its top performers by offering competitive and equitable pay, boosting employee morale and reducing turnover.

In a 2023 report by *Glassdoor*, it was found that 76% of job seekers in India consider pay transparency to be an important factor when evaluating potential employers. Organizations that fail to adopt transparent pay practices risk losing out on top-tier candidates, particularly those from Generation Z and Millennials, who are more likely to prioritize fairness in compensation.

2. Fostering Trust and Engagement

Equity in pay is a fundamental driver of trust between employees and employers. When employees believe that their compensation is based on their contributions, performance, and qualifications, they are more likely to feel engaged and motivated. Transparency in pay structures enhances this trust by eliminating the secrecy surrounding salaries and pay decisions, which can often lead to resentment, disengagement, and a toxic work environment.

A 2022 *McKinsey* survey on employee engagement found that organizations with transparent pay structures saw 33% higher engagement levels compared to those with opaque pay practices. Transparency helps employees understand the criteria behind compensation decisions and ensures that promotions, raises, and bonuses are awarded based on merit and performance, rather than favoritism or bias.

Indian organizations like *Mahindra & Mahindra* have adopted transparent pay practices to ensure that employees feel valued and fairly compensated. The company has implemented structured salary bands for various roles, providing employees with clear guidelines on how their salaries are determined and how they can progress through the organization.

3. Promoting Diversity and Inclusion

One of the most significant benefits of pay equity is its ability to promote diversity and inclusion in the workplace. By ensuring that all employees are paid fairly for their work, organizations can reduce gender and caste-based disparities in compensation, which have long been a challenge in India. Pay equity policies ensure that women, people from marginalized communities, and employees from diverse backgrounds are not disadvantaged when it comes to compensation.

Infosys, another leading IT services company in India, has made strides toward promoting gender equality in pay. The company publishes annual reports on pay equity, showcasing their commitment to reducing the gender pay gap. Infosys has implemented strict policies to ensure equal pay for equal work, irrespective of gender, and has made gender diversity a key focus in its recruitment and pay policies.

In 2021, a *Deloitte* study highlighted that organizations that focus on pay equity experience 25% higher retention rates for women and 22% higher employee satisfaction overall. This is particularly relevant for Indian companies, where gender and caste disparities in compensation are often entrenched in traditional workplace cultures.

4. Legal Compliance and Risk Mitigation

With the increasing scrutiny of labor laws and workplace regulations, pay equity and transparency also play a crucial role in ensuring legal compliance and mitigating risks related to discrimination and bias. India's *Equal Remuneration Act*, which mandates equal pay for equal work regardless of gender, is one of the many regulations that aim to address pay disparity. Ensuring equity in pay helps companies avoid legal disputes and the reputational damage that can arise from accusations of unfair pay practices.

A 2020 study by *PwC India* revealed that 62% of Indian businesses were not fully compliant with the Equal Remuneration Act, especially when it came to ensuring equal pay for women in senior leadership roles. Organizations that prioritize equity and transparency in their pay structures are better positioned to comply with such laws and avoid the legal, financial, and reputational risks associated with pay discrimination.

Best Practices for Implementing Equity and Transparency in Pay Structures

1. Clear Salary Bands and Pay Grades

One of the most effective ways to ensure pay equity is to establish clear salary bands or pay grades that outline the compensation ranges for different roles within the organization. This helps prevent any salary discrepancies between employees in similar roles and ensures consistency across departments.

Organizations like *HCL Technologies* have implemented transparent salary bands to promote fairness in compensation. Employees know the salary ranges for their roles, as well as the criteria required to progress to higher pay bands. This reduces the likelihood of pay discrepancies and fosters trust between employees and management.

2. Regular Pay Audits

Regular pay audits are essential to ensure that the pay structure remains equitable over time. By conducting periodic audits, organizations can identify any existing pay gaps and take corrective action. This is particularly important in addressing gender and caste disparities in compensation.

Accenture India conducts regular pay equity audits and has a dedicated diversity and inclusion team that focuses on ensuring fairness in compensation. These audits allow the company to identify and rectify any pay gaps, making necessary adjustments to ensure that employees are paid fairly for their work.

3. Clear Communication of Pay Policies

Transparency is not just about setting pay structures—it's about clearly communicating these structures to employees. Organizations should ensure that employees understand how their pay is determined, what factors influence pay increases, and how they can progress within the organization. Regular communication regarding compensation policies fosters a sense of fairness and reduces the potential for misunderstandings.

Wipro, for example, conducts town hall meetings and workshops to educate employees on its pay structure and the factors that influence salary decisions, such as performance, tenure, and skill development. This level of transparency helps employees feel more comfortable and informed about their compensation.

4. Performance-Based Compensation

Linking pay to performance is another best practice for ensuring fairness and transparency. Organizations should implement clear performance management systems that define how performance is measured and how it impacts pay. Employees who perform well should be rewarded accordingly, while those who fall short should receive constructive feedback and opportunities to improve.

In 2022, *Larsen & Toubro (L&T)* introduced a performance-based pay system where bonuses and raises were directly linked to an individual's contribution to the company's strategic goals. This system promotes transparency, as employees are clearly aware of how their efforts impact their compensation.

Challenges in Achieving Pay Equity and Transparency in Indian Organizations

In the face of the growing recognition of the importance of pay equity and transparency, Indian organizations face several significant challenges in implementing equitable pay structures. These challenges are deeply rooted in cultural, structural, and systemic issues that require concerted efforts to address. One of the most glaring issues is the **gender pay gap**, which remains a persistent problem across various industries and sectors. According to a 2023 report by Monster India, women in India earn 19% less than men on average, with the disparity becoming more pronounced in senior roles. This gap is often attributed to a combination of factors, including societal biases, lack of representation of women in leadership positions, and occupational segregation. Women are frequently clustered in lower-paying industries or roles, which contributes to the ongoing pay disparity. So, women are often undervalued in the workplace, with limited access to opportunities for career advancement or skill development, which perpetuates the cycle of lower pay.

Added significant challenge is the **lack of standardized pay practices** across organizations. Many Indian companies still lack a formal, standardized framework for setting and managing employee compensation. This lack of structure results in inconsistencies and inequities, which can lead to employee dissatisfaction and disengagement. A 2023 study by KPMG India revealed that 50% of companies do not have a formal pay equity framework in place. Without clear guidelines, compensation decisions often become subjective, influenced by factors such as favoritism, manager biases, or outdated practices. As a result, employees may feel that their compensation does not accurately reflect their contributions, leading to frustration and a decrease in morale.

The **cultural resistance** to pay transparency also presents a significant barrier. In India, there is a deeply ingrained cultural reluctance to openly discuss salaries, especially in the context of hierarchical organizations. In many workplaces, discussing pay can be considered inappropriate or even taboo. This cultural resistance makes it difficult for organizations to implement transparent pay practices, which are essential for promoting equity. According to a 2023 survey by the Society for Human Resource Management (SHRM) India, 60% of employees are uncomfortable discussing their salaries with colleagues, which reflects the deep-seated cultural norms that discourage open conversations about compensation. This lack of transparency can lead to suspicion and resentment among employees, who may feel that their peers are being compensated unfairly or inequitably.

A distinct challenge is the **complexity of pay structures** in Indian organizations. Pay structures in India are often multifaceted, with numerous variables influencing compensation, such as geographic location, industry, experience, and skill level. This complexity can make it difficult to ensure consistency and fairness in pay decisions. For instance, employees in metropolitan cities may receive higher compensation due to the higher cost of living, while employees in smaller towns or rural areas may be paid less, even for similar roles. Also, pay structures may vary across different industries, making it hard to establish a level playing field. As a result, ensuring pay equity becomes an arduous task, as organizations must account for a variety of factors while striving to maintain fairness.

These challenges are not insurmountable, but they do require Indian organizations to make significant changes in their approach to compensation. In order to address the gender pay gap, organizations must invest in initiatives that promote diversity and inclusion, such as mentorship programs, leadership development opportunities for women, and policies that support work-life balance. Over and above, companies must ensure that they implement standardized pay practices that are based on objective criteria and are regularly reviewed for fairness and equity. Pay transparency initiatives can help break down cultural barriers and foster a more open and honest dialogue around compensation. Even so, this requires a cultural shift within organizations, where leadership must set the tone for openness and fairness.

Identically, simplifying and streamlining pay structures is another step that organizations can take to ensure transparency and equity. By implementing standardized pay scales based on industry norms, job roles, and experience levels, companies can reduce the complexity of compensation structures and ensure that employees are compensated fairly regardless of their location or background. Technology can play a significant role in automating and standardizing these processes, making it easier for organizations to manage compensation effectively and track pay equity over time.

Equity and transparency in pay structures are not only fundamental to building trust and engagement within an organization but are also critical to attracting and retaining top talent in an increasingly competitive labor market. Indian organizations that embrace transparent pay practices are better positioned to foster a culture of inclusivity, fairness, and high performance.

While challenges remain, the growing focus on pay equity in India is helping to create a more level playing field for all employees, regardless of gender, caste, or background. By adopting best practices such as clear salary bands, regular pay audits, and performance-based compensation, Indian companies can move closer to achieving true pay equity and transparency.

As the workforce continues to evolve, organizations must remain committed to creating fair and transparent pay structures that reflect the value employees bring to the table, ensuring long-term success and organizational sustainability.

11. STRATEGIES FOR REDUCING ATTRITION

Attrition refers to the natural reduction of the workforce through voluntary separations such as resignations, retirements, or deaths, without the need for layoffs or terminations. It occurs when employees leave the organization for various reasons, including personal decisions, career advancement, job dissatisfaction, or life changes. Unlike turnover, which may include both voluntary and involuntary departures, attrition typically focuses on the voluntary departure of employees.

Attrition can be both a positive and negative factor for organizations. On the positive side, it can create space for new talent, bring in fresh ideas, and reduce the need for layoffs during economic downturns. On the negative side, high attrition rates can indicate issues within the organization, such as poor management practices, inadequate work-life balance, lack of career development opportunities, or insufficient employee engagement.

Managing attrition is essential for organizations to maintain stability, retain top talent, and minimize the costs of recruiting and training new employees.

Author: *Price, J. L. (1977). The Study of Turnover. Iowa State University Press.*

Strategies for Reducing Attrition in Indian Organizations

Attrition, or employee turnover, is a critical concern for organizations across the globe, and Indian companies are no exception. High attrition rates can have a significant impact on productivity, employee morale, and the overall organizational culture. While attrition is sometimes inevitable, organizations can adopt strategies to minimize it and retain top talent. In the Indian context, where the job market is highly competitive and employees often have a broad range of options, retention strategies need to be thoughtful, employee-centric, and aligned with both individual aspirations and organizational goals.

One of the most effective strategies for reducing attrition is **enhancing employee engagement**. Engagement goes beyond mere job satisfaction and focuses on creating a deep emotional connection between employees and the organization. Engaged employees are more likely to stay with the company because they feel valued, supported, and motivated. To foster employee engagement, organizations must offer opportunities for employees to contribute meaningfully, provide recognition for their achievements, and involve them in decision-making processes. Companies like Infosys and Wipro have successfully implemented engagement programs that focus on regular feedback, recognition, and creating a sense of belonging. Creating a culture of transparency and open communication where employees feel their voices are heard is also crucial to enhancing engagement.

New key strategy is **providing career development opportunities**. One of the primary reasons employees leave their jobs is a lack of growth prospects. Offering opportunities for skill development, career advancement, and leadership training can help retain employees who are looking for continuous improvement in their professional journey. Companies like Mahindra & Mahindra and HDFC Bank have introduced robust learning and development (L&D) programs that focus on upskilling employees and preparing them for higher roles. By investing in L&D, organizations demonstrate a commitment to employees' long-term career growth, which can significantly reduce the likelihood of attrition. In the Indian context, where a large portion of the workforce is young and driven by career aspirations, offering mentorship and clearly defined career paths is essential.

Work-life balance is another critical factor influencing retention. Indian employees, especially in urban areas, often face immense pressure due to the demands of their work. The inability to manage work-life balance can lead to burnout, dissatisfaction, and ultimately, attrition. Companies that offer flexible work schedules, remote work options, and wellness programs are better positioned to reduce turnover. The

COVID-19 pandemic has underscored the importance of flexibility, with many organizations, including major IT giants like TCS and Cognizant, adopting hybrid work models. Providing a flexible work environment helps employees feel more in control of their personal and professional lives, contributing to higher job satisfaction and lower attrition rates.

Compensation and benefits play a significant role in retention. Competitive pay, bonuses, and benefits packages are key factors in ensuring that employees remain with an organization. In India, salary is often a major consideration for employees when deciding to stay or leave. Offering a fair and transparent pay structure, coupled with performance-based incentives, can motivate employees to stay and perform better. Companies should also look beyond monetary rewards and provide benefits such as health insurance, retirement plans, and other perks that enhance the overall employee experience. Providing personalized benefits that align with employees' life stages and needs—such as childcare support, educational assistance, or wellness programs—can further enhance retention.

Organizational culture and values are fundamental in retaining talent. Indian employees are increasingly seeking employers who align with their values, particularly regarding corporate social responsibility (CSR) and sustainability. Companies that embrace diversity, equity, and inclusion (DEI) initiatives and offer a supportive work environment are more likely to retain employees. For instance, companies like Flipkart and Tata Steel have cultivated a strong corporate culture that emphasizes inclusivity and social impact, resonating well with younger generations who prioritize purpose-driven work. An organization that fosters a positive, supportive, and inclusive culture not only reduces attrition but also enhances its reputation as an employer of choice.

Exit interviews are an essential tool for understanding the reasons behind attrition and improving retention strategies. By gathering honest feedback from employees who are leaving, organizations can identify patterns and address any recurring issues that may be contributing to high turnover rates. For instance, if exit interviews consistently reveal dissatisfaction with management or lack of career development, HR can take targeted actions to improve those areas. While exit interviews are often conducted after an employee has decided to leave, some companies in India are also implementing "stay interviews" to proactively understand and address any concerns that might lead to potential attrition.

Leadership and management quality also have a profound impact on employee retention. Employees often leave managers, not organizations. If employees feel unsupported, undervalued, or micromanaged by their supervisors, they are more likely to seek opportunities elsewhere. Companies must invest in training leaders to be effective communicators, empathetic listeners, and strong supporters of their teams. Leadership development programs, such as those implemented by companies like Accenture and Hindustan Unilever, focus on grooming managers who can inspire, motivate, and retain talent.

Finally, **recognition and appreciation** are vital for retaining employees. Employees who feel appreciated for their contributions are more likely to stay with the organization. Recognition can take many forms, from public acknowledgment of achievements to small tokens of appreciation such as bonuses or gifts. Creating a culture of recognition, where employees are regularly celebrated for their hard work and contributions, not only improves retention but also boosts morale and motivation.

Albeit, reducing attrition in Indian organizations requires a multifaceted approach that addresses various aspects of the employee experience. By focusing on employee engagement, career development, work-life balance, compensation, organizational culture, and leadership quality, organizations can create an environment where employees feel valued, supported, and motivated to stay. With the right strategies in place, companies can reduce turnover, enhance productivity, and foster a loyal and committed workforce.

Case Studies on Successful HR Strategies and OB Action Plans in Reducing Attrition in Indian Organizations

Indian organizations are increasingly adopting innovative human resource (HR) strategies and organizational behavior (OB) action plans to address the challenges of high attrition rates. A strong focus on employee retention has led to the implementation of various initiatives aimed at improving employee engagement, career development, work-life balance, and overall satisfaction. Below are some notable case studies of Indian organizations that have successfully implemented HR strategies and OB action plans to reduce attrition.

1. Tata Consultancy Services (TCS) - Employee Engagement and Career Development

TCS, one of India's largest IT services companies, has long been recognized for its focus on employee engagement and retention. The company's strategy revolves around providing continuous learning opportunities, promoting internal mobility, and fostering a strong organizational culture.

TCS has implemented a program called **"Tata Consultancy Services Talent Development Program"**, which provides employees with access to a wide range of training programs, skill development courses, and leadership initiatives. This initiative not only helps employees improve their technical and professional skills but also promotes career growth and upward mobility within the organization. TCS encourages employees to explore different roles across various business units, which enhances job satisfaction and reduces the likelihood of attrition.

Equally, the company has made a concerted effort to focus on work-life balance. TCS has introduced flexible work arrangements, including the option for employees to work from home and the opportunity for job sharing. These flexible policies, along with comprehensive health and wellness benefits, have contributed to lower attrition rates.

By investing in employees' career development and providing them with a healthy work-life balance, TCS has managed to maintain relatively low attrition levels Even with the competitive nature of the Indian IT sector.

2. Mahindra & Mahindra - Organizational Culture and Employee Empowerment

Mahindra & Mahindra, one of India's largest multinational corporations, is a leader in adopting organizational behavior strategies to reduce attrition. The company's **"Rise" philosophy** centers around values such as innovation, customer-centricity, sustainability, and empowerment. This philosophy is deeply embedded in the company's culture and has played a significant role in employee retention.

Mahindra's approach to employee retention emphasizes a culture of empowerment, where employees are encouraged to take ownership of their work and contribute to the decision-making process. The company has also implemented initiatives aimed at recognizing and rewarding employee contributions, including its **"Mahindra Excellence Award"** for outstanding performance.

Likewise, Mahindra focuses on promoting work-life balance through policies like flexible working hours, wellness programs, and onsite childcare. The company also offers employees the opportunity to work on various projects across the globe, which provides them with exposure to different cultures and professional environments.

Through its strong organizational culture, employee empowerment, and commitment to work-life balance, Mahindra & Mahindra has been successful in reducing attrition and retaining top talent, especially in the highly competitive automotive and manufacturing industries.

3. Infosys - Performance Management and Learning & Development

Infosys, another major player in India's IT industry, has consistently focused on performance management and learning & development to reduce attrition. The company's **"Performance and Competency Framework"** links employee performance to career progression, ensuring that top performers are recognized and rewarded with new challenges and opportunities.

Infosys places significant emphasis on skill development and continuous learning. Its **"Global Talent Program"** offers employees access to both in-house training programs and external certifications. By investing in employees' career growth and providing the necessary resources for skill enhancement, Infosys ensures that employees feel valued and have clear paths for advancement within the company.

To further enhance employee engagement, Infosys introduced a **"Stay Interview"** program, where HR leaders and managers regularly engage with employees to understand their career aspirations, concerns, and satisfaction levels. These stay interviews help the company address any issues before they lead to attrition, fostering a more supportive work environment.

By aligning performance management with career growth, offering comprehensive learning opportunities, and proactively addressing employee concerns, Infosys has significantly reduced its attrition rates, even in the face of intense competition in the IT sector.

4. Flipkart - Employee Engagement and Recognition

Flipkart, one of India's largest e-commerce platforms, has made employee engagement and recognition a cornerstone of its HR strategy. Flipkart's HR team recognizes the importance of acknowledging employees' contributions and ensuring that they feel valued.

The company has implemented several initiatives to reduce attrition, including the **"Flipkart Celebrations"** program, which recognizes employees for their achievements on both an individual and team level. These celebrations are often integrated with Flipkart's overall business performance, creating a direct link between employee efforts and organizational success.

Also, Flipkart fosters a culture of innovation and collaboration, where employees are encouraged to contribute ideas, collaborate across teams, and experiment with new ways of doing business. The company promotes open communication between leadership and employees, ensuring that employees feel connected to the organization's goals and values.

Flipkart also prioritizes work-life balance through flexible working hours and remote working options, which have become even more important in the post-pandemic era. By combining recognition with flexibility, Flipkart has managed to maintain high levels of employee satisfaction and reduce attrition.

5. HDFC Bank - Employee Benefits and Work-Life Balance

HDFC Bank has implemented a series of HR strategies to reduce attrition and enhance employee satisfaction. A major focus of the bank's retention strategy is offering **competitive compensation and benefits**, which includes not only attractive salaries but also health insurance, retirement plans, and performance-based bonuses.

The bank also places a high value on work-life balance. HDFC Bank's employees are encouraged to take regular breaks and make use of the bank's wellness programs, including stress management workshops and access to health facilities. The organization also offers flexible working hours, especially for its employees in support functions.

HDFC Bank's **Employee Recognition Program** ensures that high performers are regularly acknowledged through various awards and public recognition initiatives. By providing employees with clear recognition for their efforts, the bank enhances job satisfaction and reduces the likelihood of attrition.

Through a combination of competitive compensation, work-life balance initiatives, and employee recognition, HDFC Bank has effectively addressed the issue of attrition in the banking sector.

Indian organizations like TCS, Mahindra & Mahindra, Infosys, Flipkart, and HDFC Bank have successfully implemented HR and OB strategies to reduce attrition. Their approaches focus on employee engagement, career development, work-life balance, recognition, and competitive compensation. By creating a supportive work environment that values employees and invests in their growth, these companies have managed to retain top talent and ensure long-term organizational success. As the Indian job market continues to evolve, more organizations are likely to follow suit and adopt similar strategies to reduce attrition and improve employee satisfaction.

12. EMOTIONAL INTELLIGENCE AND SELF-AWARENESS

Emotional Intelligence (EI), also known as Emotional Quotient (EQ), is the ability to recognize, understand, and manage one's own emotions and the emotions of others. It is a critical skill for personal and professional success, particularly in leadership, communication, and conflict resolution. The five components of EI, as identified by psychologist Daniel Goleman, include self-awareness, self-regulation, motivation, empathy, and social skills. Emotional intelligence enables individuals to navigate complex social environments, build strong relationships, and respond effectively to challenges.

Self-awareness, a key component of emotional intelligence, refers to the ability to recognize and understand one's own emotions, thoughts, and behaviors. It involves being in tune with how emotions affect decisions, actions, and relationships. Self-aware individuals are conscious of their strengths and weaknesses and use this knowledge to guide their personal and professional growth.

Self-awareness plays a pivotal role in emotional intelligence, as it allows individuals to identify emotional triggers, manage stress, and make informed decisions. Self-aware employees and leaders are more adept at maintaining emotional balance in the workplace, leading to better problem-solving and interpersonal relationships.

Author: *Goleman, D. (1995). Emotional Intelligence: Why It Can Matter More Than IQ. Bantam Books.*

Emotional Intelligence and Self-Awareness in Management and Organizational Behavior

In the modern corporate world, emotional intelligence (EI) has emerged as one of the key traits for effective leadership and organizational success. Emotional intelligence is the ability to recognize, understand, manage, and influence emotions, both in oneself and in others. Self-awareness, a core component of emotional intelligence, plays a pivotal role in leadership development, team dynamics, and overall workplace efficiency. In India, where cultural diversity and complex organizational hierarchies exist, emotional intelligence and self-awareness have become indispensable in driving sustainable performance, enhancing employee engagement, and fostering a positive work culture.

Emotional Intelligence: The Core of Effective Leadership

Emotional intelligence encompasses five key components: self-awareness, self-regulation, motivation, empathy, and social skills. These components work together to help individuals navigate complex emotional dynamics in the workplace, manage interpersonal relationships, and make informed decisions under pressure.

In the Indian corporate context, emotional intelligence is crucial for leaders, especially in large organizations where diverse teams and hierarchical structures require leaders to navigate sensitive issues and ensure smooth collaboration. Leaders with high emotional intelligence can inspire trust, provide constructive feedback, and build resilient teams that can work effectively in the face of challenges.

Author's Creation

For example, Indra Nooyi, the former CEO of PepsiCo and one of India's most prominent business leaders, is often lauded for her emotional intelligence. Her ability to build relationships, understand her team's emotional needs, and make decisions that reflect empathy has been a cornerstone of her leadership success. Such emotional acumen is especially important in Indian organizations, where relationships and trust often influence business outcomes.

Self-Awareness: A Gateway to Emotional Intelligence

Self-awareness, which refers to the ability to recognize one's emotions, strengths, weaknesses, values, and impact on others, is the foundation of emotional intelligence. It enables individuals to understand how their emotions influence their behavior and interactions with others. In management and organizational behavior, self-awareness is critical for leaders who must make objective decisions and lead teams effectively.

In India, where organizational hierarchies and respect for authority play a significant role, self-awareness helps leaders navigate complex dynamics between subordinates, peers, and senior management. Leaders who are aware of their emotional responses can control their impulses and respond appropriately, which fosters respect and effective communication within teams.

For instance, Ratan Tata, the former chairman of Tata Group, is known for his self-awareness and calm demeanor in high-pressure situations. His ability to understand his emotional responses and align them with the company's values and goals made him a respected figure in the Indian corporate world. His leadership style emphasizes humility and the importance of understanding the needs of employees, customers, and stakeholders.

Self-awareness also improves conflict resolution. When managers recognize their emotions, they are less likely to react impulsively or defensively. Instead, they can assess the situation, manage their emotions, and engage in thoughtful discussions that promote resolution. This is particularly important in Indian organizations, where workplace hierarchies and cultural nuances require delicate handling of conflicts.

The Role of Emotional Intelligence and Self-Awareness in Team Management

In the Indian corporate environment, where teams are often diverse in terms of cultural background, education, and work experience, emotional intelligence and self-awareness are essential for managing team dynamics effectively. Leaders with high EI are better equipped to understand their team members' emotions, motivations, and communication styles. This awareness allows them to tailor their leadership approaches to suit individual needs and create a more inclusive work environment.

Research has shown that emotionally intelligent leaders tend to have more motivated and productive teams. A study by the Indian Institute of Management (IIM) found that leaders who practiced emotional intelligence were able to build more cohesive teams, reduce turnover, and increase employee engagement.

For example, Infosys, one of India's leading IT services firms, has long recognized the importance of emotional intelligence in leadership. The company places significant emphasis on leadership development programs that include EI training. These programs help managers become more self-aware, understand the emotions of their team members, and create a culture of mutual respect and collaboration. As a result, Infosys has successfully managed its vast workforce and maintained high employee satisfaction levels.

Enhancing Emotional Intelligence through Training and Development

Given the importance of emotional intelligence in managing teams and leading organizations, many Indian companies are investing in training programs to enhance the emotional intelligence of their employees. These programs focus on improving self-awareness, empathy, and communication skills. They help employees recognize and manage their emotions and understand the emotional cues of others.

For example, Reliance Industries offers leadership development programs that focus on building emotional intelligence, which has contributed to the success of its leadership in managing complex and diverse teams. These programs encourage self-reflection and help leaders understand the impact of their emotional responses on their team members.

That is why, self-awareness training is not limited to leadership development. Organizations like Wipro and L&T offer workshops and seminars that promote mindfulness, emotional regulation, and interpersonal effectiveness. These workshops help employees at all levels improve their emotional intelligence, thereby contributing to better team dynamics and a more harmonious workplace.

The Impact of Emotional Intelligence and Self-Awareness on Organizational Culture

Organizational culture plays a critical role in shaping employee behavior and engagement. In India, where workplace culture often revolves around respect, loyalty, and teamwork, emotional intelligence and self-awareness have a significant impact on creating a positive and inclusive culture.

Leaders with high emotional intelligence set the tone for the entire organization. They demonstrate empathy, respect, and understanding, which encourages employees to follow suit. This creates a culture of trust, openness, and collaboration, which is essential for the growth and success of the organization.

For instance, Tata Steel has built a culture based on trust and transparency, where emotional intelligence is a key value. The company's leadership encourages open communication, ensures employees feel heard, and supports their emotional well-being, which fosters a positive work environment and strengthens the organization's culture.

The Need for Emotional Intelligence and Self-Awareness in the Indian Context

In the rapidly evolving business landscape of India, emotional intelligence and self-awareness are no longer optional skills—they are essential for leaders, managers, and employees at all levels. As Indian organizations grow in size, complexity, and global reach, the ability to manage emotions effectively will determine the success of individuals and teams. By investing in the development of emotional intelligence and self-awareness, Indian companies can create a more productive, engaged, and harmonious workplace, ultimately driving long-term success and sustainability in an increasingly competitive global market.

Organizations that prioritize EI and self-awareness in their leadership development programs will likely enjoy higher employee satisfaction, improved collaboration, and greater innovation, positioning them as leaders in their respective industries.

Case Studies of Emotional Intelligence in Indian Organizations

Several Indian companies have embraced emotional intelligence and integrated it into their organizational practices, from leadership development programs to employee engagement strategies. Here are a few notable examples:

Tata Steel: Building a Culture of Empathy and Trust Tata Steel is a prime example of an Indian organization that has successfully implemented emotional intelligence in its organizational culture. The company's leadership emphasizes the importance of empathy, emotional regulation, and active listening, which are central to their leadership philosophy. The Tata Steel management believes that emotional intelligence is critical for creating a sense of trust and transparency within the organization, allowing for more effective communication across hierarchical levels.

Tata Steel has invested in leadership development programs that focus on building emotional intelligence skills, such as empathy and self-regulation. These programs aim to help leaders manage their emotional responses, understand the perspectives of others, and make balanced decisions that benefit the company and its employees.

The results have been evident in Tata Steel's strong employee retention and engagement rates. Employees feel valued and understood, leading to a more collaborative and motivated workforce. This approach has contributed to the company's long-term success and reputation as an employer of choice.

Infosys: Integrating Emotional Intelligence into Leadership Development Infosys, one of India's leading IT services companies, has integrated emotional intelligence into its leadership development programs. The company places significant emphasis on creating leaders who not only have technical expertise but also possess strong interpersonal skills, self-awareness, and emotional regulation. Infosys uses EI to identify high-potential leaders within the organization and helps them develop the necessary emotional competencies to lead diverse teams effectively.

The company's focus on emotional intelligence is also reflected in its employee engagement initiatives. Infosys conducts regular workshops on EI, mindfulness, and stress management, aiming to improve employees' emotional resilience and create a supportive work environment. As a result, Infosys has achieved high employee satisfaction rates, improved team collaboration, and reduced turnover in a highly competitive industry.

Wipro: Employee Engagement through Emotional Intelligence Wipro, another major player in India's IT sector, has been proactive in integrating emotional intelligence into its HR and OB practices. The company has implemented programs that focus on developing emotional intelligence in its workforce, including training in emotional regulation, conflict management, and communication skills. Wipro recognizes that employees who can manage their emotions effectively are more likely to be engaged, productive, and loyal.

Beyond a certain level to its leadership development programs, Wipro has introduced initiatives like the "Wipro HR 4.0" framework, which emphasizes employee well-being, mindfulness, and emotional awareness. The company has used EI to design employee engagement surveys that measure emotional factors, such as job satisfaction, stress levels, and work-life balance. These surveys help HR professionals understand employee sentiments and take proactive measures to improve overall employee experience.

The results of Wipro's focus on emotional intelligence have been apparent in its ability to build a positive work culture and foster strong relationships between employees and management. The company has seen improvements in employee engagement, retention, and performance as a result of its commitment to emotional intelligence.

Mahindra & Mahindra: The Power of Empathy in Leadership Mahindra & Mahindra, a renowned Indian multinational conglomerate, has placed a strong emphasis on emotional intelligence to cultivate empathetic leadership within the organization. The company's "Rise" philosophy, which encourages employees to challenge the status quo, think differently, and create positive change, is deeply rooted in emotional intelligence principles. The company promotes empathy as a core leadership quality, enabling leaders to connect with their teams on an emotional level and understand their challenges.

Mahindra's leadership development programs incorporate EI training, helping managers improve their ability to recognize and manage their emotions, as well as those of their teams. This approach has not only enhanced individual leadership effectiveness but also contributed to fostering a more inclusive and supportive work environment. As a result, Mahindra & Mahindra has enjoyed high employee morale and loyalty, particularly in an industry that is heavily reliant on innovation and cross-functional collaboration.

HDFC Bank: Emotional Intelligence in Customer Service and Leadership HDFC Bank, one of India's leading private-sector banks, has integrated emotional intelligence into its HR and customer service practices. The bank's leadership development programs focus on emotional competencies such as empathy, communication, and self-regulation to create leaders who can manage stress and lead with emotional awareness. HDFC Bank has also introduced emotional intelligence as a key metric in employee performance assessments, ensuring that leaders and teams maintain strong interpersonal relationships and contribute positively to the organizational culture.

In terms of customer service, HDFC Bank uses emotional intelligence to train employees to respond to customer needs with empathy and understanding. This focus on emotional intelligence has helped the bank maintain strong customer relationships, increase customer satisfaction, and enhance its brand image.

The Impact of Emotional Intelligence on Organizational Behavior in India

The growing emphasis on emotional intelligence in Indian organizations has led to several significant changes in organizational behavior. Companies that have successfully implemented EI strategies have witnessed improvements in various aspects of organizational performance, including:

- **Increased Employee Engagement and Retention:** Leaders who are emotionally intelligent are better able to understand the needs and concerns of their employees, leading to higher levels of engagement, job satisfaction, and loyalty. By fostering a culture of empathy and emotional awareness, Indian companies have been able to reduce attrition rates and create more committed workforces.

- **Improved Collaboration and Communication:** High EI in leaders promotes open communication and transparency, leading to stronger team dynamics and better collaboration. In diverse Indian workplaces, where cultural differences can sometimes create challenges, emotional intelligence helps leaders bridge gaps and facilitate productive dialogue among team members.

- **Enhanced Leadership Effectiveness:** Leaders with high emotional intelligence are more adaptable, resilient, and capable of making balanced decisions under pressure. This leads to more effective leadership and a positive influence on organizational culture, particularly in large and complex Indian organizations.

- **Conflict Resolution and Workplace Harmony:** EI enables leaders and employees to manage conflicts constructively, reducing tensions and fostering a harmonious work environment. This is particularly important in Indian organizations, where hierarchical structures and cultural differences can sometimes lead to misunderstandings and disputes.

The Growing Significance of Emotional Intelligence in Indian Organizations

Emotional intelligence is no longer just a "soft skill" but a critical asset that can drive organizational success. In the

Indian corporate environment, where relationships, cultural nuances, and effective communication are highly valued, emotional intelligence plays a pivotal role in shaping HR practices and organizational behavior. Companies that invest in developing emotional intelligence at all levels of the organization, from leadership to employees, are better positioned to succeed in today's dynamic and competitive business landscape.

As Indian organizations continue to expand, innovate, and evolve, emotional intelligence will remain a key factor in shaping workplace culture, enhancing performance, and fostering long-term success. The case studies of companies like Tata Steel, Infosys, Wipro, Mahindra & Mahindra, and HDFC Bank demonstrate that integrating emotional intelligence into HR and OB practices can lead to significant benefits for both employees and organizations.

---

13. BUILDING HIGH-PERFORMING TEAMS

High-performing teams are groups of individuals who work collaboratively towards a shared vision, achieving exceptional results through strong communication, trust, accountability, and mutual respect. These teams possess the ability to achieve goals more effectively and efficiently than others, often exceeding expectations in both performance and innovation. The key to high performance lies in the collective contributions of team members who are empowered, motivated, and have clear roles within the team.

According to Katzenbach and Smith (1993), high-performing teams have several characteristics, including a compelling direction, a shared purpose, complementary skills, mutual accountability, and strong interpersonal relationships. These teams are typically marked by their ability to adapt to challenges, make decisions quickly, and maintain focus on achieving their objectives.

In the workplace, high-performing teams are often led by strong, supportive leaders who provide guidance and facilitate open communication. Team members are committed to each other's success, and the team culture encourages continuous learning and growth.

Effective collaboration, diversity of thought, and alignment of individual goals with team objectives are also essential for high performance. Companies that foster such environments—where employees can work cohesively and draw on their unique skills and perspectives—often see improved productivity, innovation, and employee satisfaction.

Author: *Katzenbach, J. R., & Smith, D. K. (1993). The Wisdom of Teams: Creating the High-Performance Organization. Harper Business.*

Building High-Performing Teams: Strategies and Insights for Indian Organizations

Building high-performing teams is one of the most important goals for HR and organizational leaders in any country, including India. In the dynamic and competitive Indian corporate landscape, organizations are increasingly focusing on creating teams that not only work efficiently but also innovate, collaborate, and contribute meaningfully to organizational goals. High-performing teams are characterized by a strong sense of purpose, mutual trust, open communication, and the ability to deliver exceptional results consistently.

In India, where diverse cultural backgrounds, hierarchical structures, and rapid technological advancements play a significant role in shaping the workforce, the process of building high-performing teams requires a unique approach. The following outlines strategies, best practices, and case studies on building high-performing teams within Indian organizations, especially in the context of HR and Organizational Behavior (OB).

1. Aligning Teams with Organizational Vision and Values

The foundation of any high-performing team begins with aligning team objectives with the broader organizational vision and values. Indian organizations that focus on creating a clear and shared sense of purpose provide teams with direction and motivation, ensuring that everyone is working towards a common goal.

For instance, **Mahindra & Mahindra**, a leader in the Indian automobile sector, effectively aligns its teams with the company's "Rise" philosophy, which emphasizes the importance of challenging the status quo, thinking differently, and creating positive change. Through clear communication of the organization's goals and values, Mahindra encourages teams to embody the company's ethos, which has led to high employee engagement and collaborative success.

2. Emphasizing Collaboration Over Individual Achievement

High-performing teams thrive on collaboration, where team members are encouraged to leverage each other's strengths and skills rather than compete against one another. Indian organizations, usually known for their hierarchical structures, are increasingly shifting towards a collaborative culture, where open communication, mutual support, and shared decision-making are prioritized.

Infosys, a global IT services company, exemplifies this approach by promoting teamwork and collaboration at all levels. The company's leadership development programs focus on creating leaders who encourage collaboration across different teams and departments. By fostering an environment where individuals are motivated to work together towards common goals, Infosys has built a strong culture of high-performing teams.

Flipkart, one of India's leading e-commerce platforms, also emphasizes collaboration by breaking down silos and encouraging cross-functional teams to work together on strategic projects. By fostering a collaborative culture, Flipkart has been able to maintain its competitive edge in the fast-paced e-commerce industry.

3. Leveraging Diversity to Build Innovation

Indian teams are often culturally diverse, with team members coming from various regions, backgrounds, and ethnicities. Embracing this diversity and turning it into an asset is a powerful strategy for building high-performing teams. Diverse teams bring a wide range of perspectives, ideas, and problem-solving approaches, which can lead to more innovative and creative outcomes.

For example, **Tata Consultancy Services (TCS)** is known for leveraging its diverse workforce to drive innovation. With employees from all parts of India and across the globe, TCS fosters an inclusive culture where diverse ideas are encouraged and valued. This diversity not only enhances team dynamics but also improves problem-solving and innovation. TCS's collaborative and inclusive approach has contributed to its status as one of the largest IT services firms globally.

4. Effective Leadership and Empowerment

Effective leadership is critical in guiding high-performing teams. In India, where hierarchical leadership styles are still prevalent in many sectors, there has been a noticeable shift towards more transformational and empowering leadership models. Leaders of high-performing teams must inspire, empower, and motivate their team members to unlock their full potential.

Wipro is a great example of an Indian organization that has implemented effective leadership strategies to build high-performing teams. Wipro's leadership training programs emphasize emotional intelligence, empathy, and conflict resolution, all of which contribute to a more supportive and collaborative work environment. By focusing on empowering leaders who can foster trust and open communication, Wipro has successfully built teams that are agile, resilient, and results-driven.

5. Setting Clear Goals and Expectations

Setting clear, measurable goals is essential for high-performing teams. Teams need to know what is expected of them and how their performance will be evaluated. In Indian organizations, the use of Key Performance Indicators (KPIs) and Objectives and Key Results (OKRs) has become increasingly popular to measure team performance.

Byju's, the Indian edtech giant, has effectively implemented OKRs to drive performance and ensure alignment across its teams. By setting ambitious yet achievable objectives and tracking key results, Byju's has created an environment of accountability and continuous improvement. This clear focus on measurable outcomes has led to high levels of performance and innovation, helping Byju's maintain its leadership position in the competitive edtech industry.

Similarly, **HDFC Bank** uses well-defined KPIs to measure the performance of its teams and ensure that everyone is aligned with the bank's strategic objectives. By setting clear expectations and holding teams accountable, HDFC Bank fosters a high-performance culture across its various divisions.

6. Continuous Learning and Development

Continuous learning and upskilling are vital components of high-performing teams. In India's rapidly changing business environment, organizations must invest in ongoing learning to ensure that their teams have the skills and knowledge to adapt to new challenges and technologies.

Indian companies are increasingly offering personalized training programs and learning opportunities to their employees. For instance, **Zee Entertainment** provides its employees with access to platforms like LinkedIn Learning and EdCast, offering personalized learning and development pathways. By empowering teams with the resources to develop new skills, Zee Entertainment ensures that employees stay relevant and continue to contribute to high performance.

Besides, **Reliance Industries** has embraced continuous learning by providing employees with access to a wide range of internal and external training programs. This focus on professional development has helped the company build high-performing teams that are adaptable, innovative, and well-equipped to handle the challenges of the future.

7. Recognition and Rewards

Recognizing and rewarding team achievements is an essential element of building and sustaining high-performing teams. In India, where employee loyalty and job security are often highly valued, recognition and rewards play a key role in fostering a motivated and engaged workforce.

Deloitte India is an example of an organization that effectively uses recognition and rewards to build high-performing teams. The company has implemented various recognition programs that celebrate individual and team achievements. This not only boosts employee morale but also encourages teams to strive for excellence and exceed expectations.

Likewise, **Accenture India** uses both financial and non-financial rewards to motivate its employees and teams. Regular recognition, combined with career advancement opportunities and performance-based incentives, helps keep teams engaged and focused on their objectives.

8. Psychological Safety and Trust

Psychological safety is crucial for high-performing teams. Employees must feel safe to take risks, make mistakes, and voice their opinions without fear of judgment or retribution. In Indian organizations, where hierarchical relationships often exist, creating a psychologically safe environment can be challenging, but it is essential for fostering innovation and high performance.

Google India is an example of a company that promotes psychological safety within teams. Google's leadership encourages open communication, active listening, and feedback, ensuring that employees feel comfortable sharing ideas and suggestions. This open and transparent culture has allowed Google to build teams that are highly innovative and collaborative, driving the company's success in India.

Building High-Performing Teams in the Indian Corporate Context

Building high-performing teams in Indian organizations requires a blend of effective leadership, clear goals, collaboration, continuous learning, and recognition. Indian companies are increasingly adopting global best practices while tailoring them to fit their unique cultural and organizational contexts. By embracing these strategies, organizations can create high-performing teams that not only achieve exceptional results but also contribute to a positive and dynamic work culture.

As the business environment continues to evolve, organizations in India must focus on nurturing teams that can adapt, innovate, and collaborate. Through a strategic approach to team building, companies can unlock the full potential of their workforce and drive long-term success in an increasingly competitive global market.

Structure and Requirements for High-Performing Teams

High-performing teams are the cornerstone of successful organizations, driving innovation, efficiency, and achieving exceptional results. To create and sustain high-performing teams, organizations must understand the core elements of team structure and the essential requirements needed to maximize the team's potential. This requires a combination of strategic planning, leadership, clear communication, a culture of trust, and continuous development.

Here's a breakdown of the key structural components and requirements that form the foundation of high-performing teams:

1. Clear Team Objectives and Goals

A high-performing team begins with a clear understanding of its mission, objectives, and desired outcomes. This ensures that all team members are aligned with the organization's broader vision and strategic goals. When objectives are clearly defined, it allows for a focus on measurable results and drives motivation among the team members.

In Indian organizations, setting specific, measurable, achievable, relevant, and time-bound (SMART) goals is a fundamental practice. Teams must understand how their individual contributions directly tie into the larger organizational objectives. For instance, Tata Consultancy Services (TCS) ensures that each team sets individual and collective goals in alignment with their business goals, which helps to track progress effectively and enables clear focus.

2. Effective Leadership and Clear Direction

Leadership is critical to the success of any team. High-performing teams require leaders who can provide clear direction, inspire the team, and make critical decisions when needed. Effective leadership also includes fostering a culture of openness, accountability, and trust, empowering team members to contribute their ideas and insights.

Indian organizations, such as Wipro and Infosys, understand that transformational leadership plays a pivotal role in motivating teams to perform at their best. Leaders should not only set clear expectations but also encourage team members to take ownership of their work, make decisions, and share responsibility for the team's success.

3. Diverse and Complementary Skillsets

One of the core requirements for high-performing teams is diversity in skills, expertise, and perspectives. Teams are most effective when they include individuals with varied strengths and complementary abilities. By integrating diverse perspectives and expertise, teams can approach problems from multiple angles, fostering creativity and better decision-making.

In the Indian corporate context, companies such as Infosys and Flipkart embrace diversity in their teams by hiring individuals from different backgrounds, with varying skill sets and experiences. This diverse skillset ensures that teams can tackle complex problems and innovate in ways that a homogenous group might not be able to.

4. Trust and Psychological Safety

Trust is the foundation of high-performing teams. Team members must feel confident that their colleagues will support them and collaborate effectively. This trust is built through transparent communication, mutual respect, and consistent actions.

Psychological safety is equally essential, as it allows team members to take risks, make mistakes, and express their opinions without fear of judgment or retaliation. When individuals feel safe to speak up, they are more likely to contribute valuable ideas, challenge the status quo, and collaborate openly.

Zee Entertainment has been particularly focused on building psychological safety in its teams. By encouraging open feedback, transparency, and trust, Zee Entertainment ensures its teams are innovative, accountable, and resilient.

5. Clear Roles and Responsibilities

Clearly defined roles and responsibilities are essential for preventing confusion and ensuring that each team member understands what is expected of them. High-performing teams work best when everyone knows their individual responsibilities and the collective outcomes they are working towards.

For Indian organizations such as Mahindra & Mahindra, clarity in role distribution is vital to avoid overlaps and confusion. In cross-functional teams, it's particularly important that each person knows their specific deliverables, which contribute to the team's success.

6. Effective Communication

Communication is at the heart of every successful team. High-performing teams require open, transparent, and regular communication between team members. This includes both formal and informal communication channels to ensure that everyone is on the same page and that concerns are addressed quickly.

In organizations like Accenture India, clear and continuous communication is encouraged at all levels. This includes regular check-ins, meetings, and feedback loops. Effective communication ensures that team members feel heard, that decisions are well-explained, and that everyone is aligned with the overall objectives.

7. Collaboration and Cooperation

Collaboration involves working together towards common goals and leveraging each team member's strengths. High-performing teams foster an environment where individuals are not just working in silos but are actively collaborating with one another. This allows for the free exchange of ideas, peer learning, and collective problem-solving.

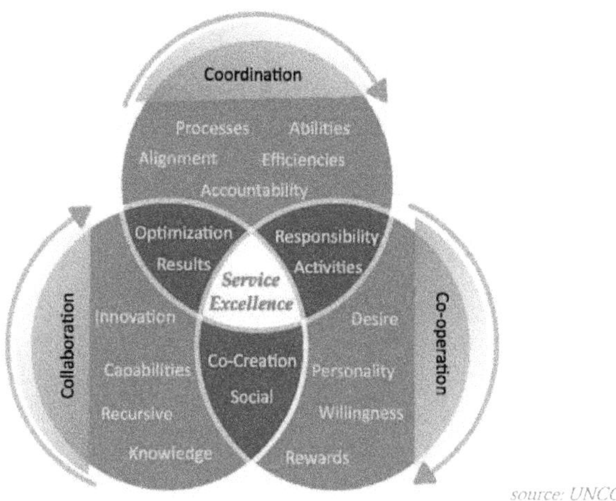

source: UNCG

Reliance Industries encourages a collaborative approach by having cross-functional teams that are tasked with specific objectives but must cooperate with other departments to achieve them. The collaborative culture in Reliance has helped foster innovation, solve complex problems, and deliver high-quality results.

8. Recognition and Reward Systems

Recognition and reward systems are crucial to maintaining high levels of motivation and morale within teams. Acknowledging individual and collective achievements ensures that team members feel valued and appreciated for their contributions. Recognition can take the form of verbal praise, performance-based bonuses, or public acknowledgment in team meetings.

Organizations like Deloitte India have adopted recognition programs that celebrate team and individual accomplishments, from awards ceremonies to quarterly recognition programs. This serves as both motivation and reinforcement, encouraging team members to continue performing at their best.

9. Continuous Learning and Development

High-performing teams are built on the foundation of continuous growth. Organizations need to invest in training and development programs that allow team members to improve their skills, adapt to changing business needs, and remain competitive in their roles.

In India, Wipro and Infosys both prioritize continuous learning by offering extensive professional development programs. These programs focus on both technical skills and soft skills, ensuring that teams remain adaptable, innovative, and capable of meeting future challenges.

Too, AI-based learning tools and e-learning platforms such as LinkedIn Learning and EdCast are increasingly being utilized by Indian corporates to deliver personalized learning experiences that cater to the evolving needs of team members.

10. Data-Driven Performance Management

A data-driven approach to performance management can provide real-time insights into team dynamics and individual contributions. By using tools like Key Performance Indicators (KPIs) and Objectives and Key Results (OKRs), organizations can track progress, identify gaps, and make data-informed decisions on resource allocation, training, and development.

Byju's, the leading ed-tech company, uses OKRs to align its teams with business goals and ensure that performance is measurable and transparent. Similarly, HDFC Bank uses KPIs to assess individual and team performance, making data-driven decisions that promote a high level of accountability and focus.

11. Resilience and Adaptability

Finally, high-performing teams need to be resilient and adaptable to navigate challenges, market changes, and unforeseen circumstances. Resilience involves maintaining focus and motivation Even with setbacks, while adaptability ensures that teams can pivot when necessary, especially in dynamic environments.

14.   BUILDING INCLUSIVE CULTURES

An inclusive culture refers to a workplace environment where all employees, regardless of their background, identity, or experiences, feel valued, respected, and supported. It is characterized by practices that promote diversity, equity, and inclusion, creating a space where individuals from different gender, racial, ethnic, and socio-economic backgrounds can thrive. In an inclusive culture, employees have equal access to opportunities, resources, and support, leading to a sense of belonging and participation.

Shore et al. (2011) define an inclusive culture as one where "individual differences are not only accepted but are celebrated as valuable to the organization." In this culture, leadership is committed to creating an environment where everyone feels they can contribute without fear of bias, exclusion, or discrimination.

Inclusive organizations take active steps to dismantle barriers and challenge biases that may exist at all levels of the organization, from hiring practices to daily operations. These steps include creating policies to ensure fair treatment, implementing diversity training, and forming employee resource groups (ERGs) that provide spaces for underrepresented groups to connect and share experiences.

An inclusive culture benefits both employees and the organization. For employees, it means they can be their authentic selves and contribute fully to their teams. For the organization, an inclusive culture fosters innovation, increases employee engagement, improves retention, and strengthens its reputation.

Author: *Shore, L. M., Cleveland, J. N., & Sanchez, D. (2011). Inclusive workplaces: A review and model. Human Resource Management Review, 21(1), 3-10.*

In the context of Organizational Behavior (OB) and Human Resources (HR), an inclusive culture is defined as an organizational environment where every employee, regardless of their demographic characteristics, identity, or background, is treated with respect, valued for their unique contributions, and provided equal opportunities to thrive. It is a workplace culture where diversity is recognized as a strength and actively promoted, ensuring that employees feel safe, supported, and empowered to be their authentic selves.

From an **OB perspective**, inclusive culture involves creating an organizational climate where individuals are recognized not only for their skills and expertise but also for their diverse perspectives, backgrounds, and experiences. The focus is on ensuring that every member of the organization can contribute meaningfully, engage in open communication, and participate in decision-making processes. Inclusive culture directly impacts employee motivation, job satisfaction, commitment, and organizational performance, as it fosters a sense of belonging and acceptance, which leads to higher levels of engagement and productivity.

From an **HR perspective**, an inclusive culture is embedded in policies, practices, and procedures that promote fairness, equity, and transparency. HR plays a pivotal role in shaping and maintaining such a culture by developing inclusive hiring practices, offering training programs focused on diversity and inclusion, implementing policies that support work-life balance and employee well-being, and ensuring that all employees have access to growth and advancement opportunities without facing discrimination or bias. HR leaders are responsible for driving awareness about unconscious biases, creating safe spaces for dialogue, and fostering an environment where everyone's contributions are recognized and rewarded equitably.

In essence, an inclusive culture in OB and HR is about ensuring that all employees, irrespective of their gender, race, ethnicity, sexual orientation, disability, or other characteristics, feel valued, included, and empowered within the organization. This culture ultimately enhances team dynamics, drives innovation, and leads to higher overall organizational success.

An **inclusive culture** refers to a workplace environment where all employees, regardless of their gender, age, race, ethnicity, sexual orientation, disability, or other personal characteristics, feel respected, valued, and empowered to fully participate in all aspects of work. In an inclusive culture, diversity is not just accepted but embraced as a key asset, and every individual is provided equal opportunities to contribute, grow, and thrive.

Key aspects of an inclusive culture include:

1. **Respect for Diversity**: An inclusive culture acknowledges and celebrates differences among employees, fostering an environment where diverse perspectives, backgrounds, and experiences are valued. This diversity could relate to gender, ethnicity, education, religion, cultural background, and more.

2. **Equality of Opportunity**: In an inclusive culture, all employees are given equal opportunities for career advancement, learning, and development. This includes equal access to promotions, training, and mentoring regardless of an individual's background.

3. **Supportive Environment**: Employees in an inclusive culture are supported in balancing their work and personal lives, as well as addressing any challenges related to their identity or personal circumstances. Policies such as flexible work hours, maternity leave, and employee assistance programs often play a role here.

4. **A Voice for Everyone**: An inclusive culture encourages open dialogue and ensures that all employees feel comfortable expressing their opinions, concerns, and suggestions without fear of discrimination or retaliation. Employees are actively involved in decision-making processes.

5. **Leadership Commitment**: Strong leadership commitment is crucial to driving inclusivity. Leaders should model inclusive behavior, hold others accountable, and actively

work to create policies that promote equality and inclusion.

6. **Continuous Learning**: An inclusive culture promotes ongoing education and awareness around issues of diversity, equity, and inclusion. This includes training programs, discussions, and events that help employees understand and challenge their biases and assumptions.

In an inclusive culture, employees feel a sense of belonging and are motivated to bring their authentic selves to work, leading to higher levels of engagement, collaboration, and innovation. Ultimately, an inclusive culture not only enhances individual and organizational performance but also drives long-term success by fostering a supportive and diverse workplace.

Creating and maintaining an inclusive culture in organizations, especially within the context of India's complex and diverse social fabric, comes with its unique set of challenges. Even with the clear benefits that such a culture offers, organizations often face multiple barriers that impede their efforts to build inclusive environments. These challenges stem from a variety of factors, such as unconscious biases, resistance to change, and deeply rooted societal norms, and they manifest in different forms across sectors and levels within the organization.

One of the most significant challenges is unconscious bias. This bias, though often unintentional, can influence key organizational processes such as decision-making, recruitment, promotions, and day-to-day interactions within teams. These biases often lead to discrimination or the marginalization of certain groups, undermining an organization's efforts to foster diversity and inclusion. For example, unconscious bias may affect how hiring managers perceive candidates from underrepresented backgrounds, leading to less diverse hiring choices or career advancement opportunities for those groups.

Alternative obstacle is resistance to change, particularly within organizations with long-established hierarchies and rigid practices. Employees, especially those in leadership roles, may resist adopting inclusive policies out of fear of losing power or privilege. This resistance can also stem from a misunderstanding of the true value of diversity and inclusion or a reluctance to challenge the status quo. Overcoming this resistance requires clear, continuous communication about the benefits of inclusivity and a shift in organizational culture to embrace change at every level.

The lack of awareness and education about the importance of an inclusive culture is also a significant barrier. In many cases, employees and leaders may not fully understand the core principles of diversity, equity, and inclusion, or how these principles impact organizational success. Without regular training and clear communication on these issues, employees may fail to actively work to address biases or engage in inclusive behaviors, further hindering progress. Education initiatives should go beyond one-time training sessions and become embedded into the organizational culture, ensuring that all employees understand how to promote and practice inclusivity.

Cultural and societal norms also play a major role in the challenges of fostering an inclusive culture. India's diverse social landscape, marked by traditional beliefs and biases around caste, gender, religion, and other factors, can influence workplace behavior and dynamics. Employees from marginalized groups may experience exclusion or bias due to these entrenched societal attitudes, which often spill over into the workplace. Addressing these deep-rooted issues requires ongoing efforts to challenge societal norms and change individual mindsets, which can take time and consistent leadership commitment.

Limited representation in leadership is another challenge that many organizations face when trying to create an inclusive culture. If leadership teams do not reflect the diversity of the broader employee base, it sends a message that certain groups are not valued or considered for leadership roles. This lack of representation also limits the effectiveness of inclusion initiatives, as those in leadership may not fully understand the challenges faced by underrepresented employees. Encouraging diversity in leadership positions requires intentional efforts such as mentorship programs, equitable opportunities for career advancement, and leadership training for diverse employees.

Inequitable opportunities for growth and development persist in many organizations, In the face of the presence of diversity policies. Employees from marginalized backgrounds may still face barriers in accessing training, promotions, and fair compensation, which can undermine the inclusivity efforts of the organization. These inequities often contribute to high turnover rates among underrepresented groups, as they feel that their potential is not being fully recognized or supported.

Communication barriers in diverse organizations can also create challenges to fostering an inclusive culture. Language differences, cultural misunderstandings, and varying communication styles can hinder effective collaboration and teamwork. These barriers can contribute to divisions between employees, limiting their ability to work cohesively and diminishing overall organizational performance. Encouraging open communication, team-building activities, and intercultural training are essential steps toward overcoming these challenges.

Tokenism, where organizations promote diversity initiatives for appearances without embedding meaningful changes in their practices or culture, is another significant challenge. Tokenism occurs when employees from diverse backgrounds are included in teams or leadership positions but are not given equal opportunities to contribute or influence decision-making. This approach undermines trust and damages employee morale, leading to feelings of resentment and frustration among employees who feel their contributions are not truly valued.

Inadequate feedback and accountability mechanisms can further hinder the success of inclusion initiatives. Without robust channels for employees to provide feedback on diversity and inclusion efforts, it becomes difficult for organizations to assess the effectiveness of their programs and identify areas that need improvement. If employees do not feel safe expressing their concerns about exclusion or discrimination, the organization may fail to address issues that negatively impact the culture and employee satisfaction.

Finally, a lack of support for diverse employees can lead to isolation and disengagement. For example, employees with disabilities may not receive the accommodations they need, or those from underrepresented groups may lack mentorship or sponsorship opportunities, which are crucial for career advancement. Providing comprehensive support systems for diverse employees is essential to ensure they feel valued and empowered in the organization. This can include flexible work arrangements, mentorship programs, and employee resource groups that offer support and development opportunities.

To overcome these challenges, organizations must take a multi-faceted approach. This includes committing to long-term efforts such as ongoing education on diversity, implementing policies that address biases, providing equitable opportunities for career development, and fostering an environment where diversity and inclusion are woven into the organizational values. With consistent effort from leadership and engagement at all levels, organizations can create an inclusive culture that attracts, retains, and empowers employees from all backgrounds, ultimately driving greater innovation, employee satisfaction, and organizational success.

Building Inclusive Cultures in Organizations

In today's dynamic business environment, building an inclusive culture is not only a moral imperative but also a strategic necessity. Inclusive cultures foster diverse perspectives, which can drive innovation, enhance employee engagement, and improve organizational performance. As India continues to evolve as a global business hub, companies that embrace inclusivity and diversity will be better positioned to attract top talent, retain employees, and succeed in an increasingly competitive marketplace.

Inclusion goes beyond simply having a diverse workforce. It is about creating an environment where every individual feels valued, respected, and has equal access to opportunities for growth, advancement, and contribution. Building such a culture requires intentional strategies, consistent effort, and leadership commitment to inclusivity.

1. Leadership Commitment to Inclusion

The foundation of any inclusive culture begins with strong leadership commitment. Leaders must not only champion diversity and inclusion but also lead by example. This involves creating a vision for diversity and inclusion that aligns with the organization's values and mission. In India, where traditional hierarchical structures may exist, top leadership's support is critical to ensuring that inclusion is prioritized across all levels of the organization.

Leaders like **Natarajan Chandrasekaran**, the Chairman of Tata Group, have been instrumental in embedding diversity and inclusion in the corporate culture of Tata Group. Under his leadership, Tata Group has taken significant steps to

176

promote gender diversity, social inclusion, and equal opportunities, ensuring that their workforce reflects India's diverse society.

2. Diverse and Inclusive Recruitment Practices

An inclusive culture begins with inclusive recruitment practices. Organizations must make conscious efforts to attract diverse talent, not only in terms of gender, but also considering race, caste, age, disability, and other factors. In India, this requires overcoming traditional biases in hiring and ensuring that recruitment practices are free from discrimination.

For instance, **Accenture India** has implemented inclusive hiring practices by recruiting from a wide pool of talent, including those from non-traditional backgrounds, persons with disabilities, and women returning to work after a career break. The company has introduced special programs to ensure that all applicants, regardless of their background, have equal opportunities to succeed.

Hence, companies like **Flipkart** use AI-driven recruitment tools to remove unconscious biases during the hiring process, ensuring that candidates are evaluated based solely on their skills and potential.

3. Creating Safe Spaces for Open Dialogue

A key component of an inclusive culture is the establishment of safe spaces where employees can share their experiences, express concerns, and engage in open dialogue about diversity and inclusion issues. These conversations allow employees to feel heard and supported, and they help the organization address any systemic issues or barriers that may exist.

Companies such as **Cognizant Technology Solutions** have implemented programs that provide a platform for employees to voice their concerns around diversity and inclusion, whether it's gender, sexual orientation, or racial identity. These initiatives are designed to make employees feel safe and encourage them to be open about the challenges they face in the workplace. This fosters a sense of belonging and support, critical for inclusive engagement.

4. Training and Education on Diversity and Inclusion

Training programs focused on diversity and inclusion are essential for raising awareness and changing mindsets within the organization. In India, where cultural and social dynamics often create biases, training sessions that address topics such as unconscious bias, cultural sensitivity, and gender equality are essential for creating an inclusive environment.

Infosys offers workshops and e-learning courses on diversity, equity, and inclusion as part of its broader strategy to create a more inclusive workplace. These programs are designed not only for new hires but also for existing employees, ensuring that everyone is equipped with the knowledge and skills to foster an inclusive culture.

5. Mentorship and Sponsorship Programs

Mentorship and sponsorship programs are key to advancing diversity and inclusion in organizations. Such programs provide support to underrepresented groups, helping them navigate career challenges, gain visibility, and access opportunities for growth. Mentorship creates a more equitable environment where individuals from diverse backgrounds can receive guidance from more experienced colleagues.

Mahindra & Mahindra, with its focus on gender diversity, has established mentorship programs to support women in leadership roles. These initiatives aim to nurture female talent and provide them with the necessary skills and confidence to take on leadership positions.

6. Employee Resource Groups (ERGs) and Affinity Networks

Employee Resource Groups (ERGs) are another powerful tool in fostering inclusivity. ERGs are voluntary, employee-led groups that are formed based on shared characteristics or experiences such as gender, ethnicity, disability, or sexual orientation. These groups provide a sense of community and allow employees to connect with others who share similar experiences.

IBM India has a well-established network of ERGs, such as Women at IBM, that help support its employees' needs and create a more inclusive environment. These groups are instrumental in driving initiatives that promote work-life balance, gender equity, and social justice.

7. Equitable Opportunities for Career Development

In an inclusive culture, all employees must have equitable access to opportunities for career development, advancement, and skill-building. Organizations need to ensure that employees from diverse backgrounds are not only given equal opportunities for promotions but are also supported through training and development programs to enhance their skillsets.

Companies like **Wipro** and **HCL Technologies** have designed leadership development programs that focus on identifying and nurturing high-potential individuals from diverse backgrounds. These programs ensure that the next generation of leaders reflects the diversity of the broader workforce and society.

8. Promoting Gender Diversity and Inclusion

Gender diversity remains one of the most pressing issues in building an inclusive culture, especially in India, where traditional gender roles still influence workplace dynamics. Promoting gender diversity requires creating an environment where women feel supported, respected, and have equal opportunities to thrive in their careers.

Tata Consultancy Services (TCS) is one of the pioneers in promoting gender diversity, with initiatives aimed at improving women's representation in leadership roles. TCS has implemented flexible work policies, such as work-from-home options, to support women, particularly those balancing work and family responsibilities. This has helped the company not only retain female talent but also promote them into senior leadership positions.

9. Regular Monitoring and Feedback

Creating an inclusive culture is an ongoing process that requires continuous monitoring and feedback. Organizations must regularly assess the effectiveness of their diversity and inclusion initiatives and make data-driven decisions to improve inclusivity. Collecting feedback from employees through surveys, focus groups, and one-on-one discussions helps the company understand the impact of its efforts and identify areas for improvement.

HDFC Bank regularly conducts employee engagement surveys and feedback sessions to understand the inclusivity of its workplace culture. The bank uses this feedback to refine its diversity strategies and ensure that the workplace remains welcoming and equitable for all employees.

10. Celebrating Diversity

Finally, celebrating diversity through various cultural and social events is essential in building an inclusive culture. These celebrations provide opportunities for employees to share their backgrounds, traditions, and experiences, which enhances mutual understanding and respect.

Cognizant has an annual Diversity Day where employees from different backgrounds come together to celebrate cultural diversity. These events help raise awareness about various cultures and traditions and promote an environment where everyone feels accepted and valued.

Building an inclusive culture is a long-term commitment that requires deliberate actions, leadership support, and a deep understanding of the challenges and barriers that different groups face.

15. MEASURING DEI SUCCESS

Diversity, Equity, and Inclusion (DEI) are critical components of organizational culture, especially in today's globalized and increasingly diverse workforce. These three interconnected concepts—Diversity, Equity, and Inclusion—represent the ongoing efforts to create more inclusive, fair, and equal workplaces. Each aspect has its own unique focus, but together they work toward creating a balanced and supportive environment for all employees.

Diversity, Equity, and Inclusion (DEI) in Indian Organizations

The concepts of Diversity, Equity, and Inclusion (DEI) are integral to building strong, progressive organizations. They work in tandem to create environments where employees can thrive, contribute, and feel valued, regardless of their background or personal characteristics. In the context of Indian organizations, DEI is particularly significant due to the country's unique social fabric, which is characterized by diversity across caste, gender, language, and religion. Understanding and embracing these principles is crucial for organizations aiming for sustainable growth, innovation, and employee engagement.

Diversity

Diversity within an organization refers to the recognition and celebration of differences among employees. This includes not only visible traits such as gender, ethnicity, and age but also invisible traits like educational background, socioeconomic status, disability, sexual orientation, and professional experience. In the Indian context, diversity extends beyond the conventional dimensions to encompass regional, linguistic, and cultural differences. Given the country's vastness and complex social structure, organizations are increasingly realizing the need to promote diversity to reflect the broader population and appeal to global and domestic markets.

For instance, companies like Infosys and Wipro have made significant strides in promoting gender diversity, ensuring that underrepresented groups have a voice within the workforce. These companies have instituted policies to increase the recruitment and retention of women and have introduced programs aimed at leadership development for women. Too, diversity in educational and professional experiences is also a focal point for these organizations, allowing them to tap into a wide range of perspectives and skills.

In sectors like technology and consulting, where innovation and creative problem-solving are critical, the presence of diverse perspectives allows for better decision-making and problem-solving. By encouraging diversity, organizations can create more dynamic teams capable of tackling complex challenges and coming up with innovative solutions.

Equity

Equity goes beyond diversity by ensuring that all employees have equal access to opportunities and resources, regardless of their background or identity. In the workplace, equity involves identifying and addressing systemic barriers that prevent certain groups from advancing or achieving their potential. Unlike equality, which offers everyone the same resources or opportunities, equity takes into account the different starting points of individuals and aims to level the playing field by providing the resources and opportunities that meet their specific needs.

In India, equity is an especially important issue due to the persistence of caste, gender, and regional biases in many sectors. Disparities in hiring, promotions, and compensation practices can create inequality, even within diverse organizations. Companies like Accenture and Cognizant have been pioneers in implementing pay equity programs, ensuring that all employees receive equal pay for equal work, regardless of their gender or background. Over and above, these organizations have rolled out career development programs designed to help employees from underrepresented groups advance in their careers by offering mentorship and leadership training opportunities.

Equity also plays a role in shaping the company's policies for work-life balance, access to professional development resources, and opportunities for career advancement. By focusing on equity, organizations can help remove the barriers that prevent employees from marginalized or historically disadvantaged groups from thriving in their careers.

Inclusion

Inclusion is about creating a workplace where all employees feel valued, respected, and integrated into the organizational culture. It's not just about hiring diverse employees but actively creating a supportive environment where everyone can participate and contribute meaningfully. Inclusion in the workplace ensures that employees from all backgrounds have equal opportunities to engage, voice their opinions, and access growth opportunities.

Creating an inclusive environment requires leadership commitment to ensuring that all employees, regardless of their identity or background, feel they belong. This can include implementing policies that prevent discrimination, providing platforms for open dialogue, and supporting employee resource groups (ERGs). Organizations like Mahindra & Mahindra and Flipkart have demonstrated strong efforts in fostering inclusion by introducing flexible work arrangements, mentorship programs, and diversity training sessions. These initiatives help employees navigate workplace challenges, build stronger relationships, and ensure that diverse viewpoints are integrated into the organization's decision-making processes.

Inclusion is also about addressing unconscious biases that may exist within the organization. Many companies now use tools to reduce biases in hiring, performance evaluations, and promotions. By actively working to create an inclusive culture, organizations can enhance employee morale, foster collaboration, and create an environment where everyone can contribute to their fullest potential.

Shore, L. M., Cleveland, J. N., & Sanchez, D. (2011). Inclusive workplaces: A review and model. *Human Resource Management Review, 21*(1), 3-10.

The Role of DEI in Organizational Behavior (OB)

DEI principles have a direct impact on organizational behavior (OB) as they shape the ways in which employees interact, collaborate, and work together. When organizations prioritize DEI, they create an environment where diverse individuals can collaborate effectively, share different perspectives, and drive innovation. A culture of inclusion leads to better communication, improved team dynamics, and increased overall productivity.

For example, a diverse and inclusive workforce is more likely to foster a culture of openness and collaboration. It encourages individuals to bring their whole selves to work and share their unique insights, which can lead to greater creativity and problem-solving. In turn, this enhances the organization's ability to adapt to challenges and leverage diverse strengths.

Leadership plays a crucial role in shaping the DEI culture of an organization. Inclusive leaders are proactive in creating a supportive work environment, ensuring fair opportunities for all employees, and advocating for policies that promote diversity and inclusion at all levels of the organization. When leadership demonstrates a commitment to DEI, it sends a clear message to the rest of the organization about the value placed on diversity and inclusion.

Diversity, Equity, and Inclusion are more than just buzzwords; they are foundational elements that contribute to the overall success and growth of organizations. In India, where cultural, social, and regional diversity is particularly pronounced, embracing DEI can enhance employee engagement, improve innovation, and foster a positive organizational culture. Indian companies are increasingly recognizing the importance of DEI, and many have made significant progress in implementing inclusive practices. Even with that, achieving true inclusion, equity, and diversity requires continuous effort, long-term commitment, and strong leadership to break down barriers and address biases. Organizations that succeed in integrating DEI into their culture will be better positioned to attract top talent, enhance employee satisfaction, and remain competitive in a rapidly changing global marketplace.

Why DEI Matters

The business case for DEI is compelling. Research consistently shows that diverse and inclusive teams are more innovative, productive, and successful. Organizations that prioritize DEI are better able to attract top talent, retain employees, and increase their competitive advantage. In India, with its diverse population and rapidly changing business landscape, DEI initiatives are essential for fostering creativity and addressing the complex needs of a globalized market. Not to mention, a strong DEI strategy can improve employee morale, job satisfaction, and engagement, leading to a more positive organizational culture.

The Role of DEI in Organizational Behavior (OB)

In OB, DEI plays a significant role in shaping individual and group behavior within an organization. The principles of DEI directly influence how employees interact with each other, how teams collaborate, and how leaders make decisions. When organizations prioritize DEI, they create an environment where people feel safe and supported, which encourages open communication, teamwork, and collaboration. It also helps reduce conflicts, discrimination, and harassment, leading to higher employee satisfaction and performance.

DEI also impacts leadership practices, as leaders must ensure that their teams reflect the organization's commitment to diversity and inclusion. Leaders who foster an inclusive culture can positively influence the organization's overall performance by empowering employees, encouraging creativity, and helping people from diverse backgrounds thrive.

Challenges and Failures in DEI Implementation

In the face of the positive strides made by some Indian organizations, others have faced significant challenges and failures in their DEI initiatives. These challenges often stem from a lack of commitment, insufficient understanding of DEI principles, and systemic barriers that are deeply entrenched in the Indian corporate landscape. Let's look at some common failures and barriers to DEI implementation in Indian organizations:

1. Unconscious Bias in Hiring and Promotions

One of the most significant failures in DEI initiatives across many Indian organizations is the persistence of unconscious bias, particularly in hiring and promotion practices. Many companies still face challenges in overcoming gender, caste, and regional biases in recruitment and career progression. For example, women in leadership roles often face barriers in being considered for high-level positions, particularly in male-dominated sectors like engineering and IT. This bias is often unintentional but deeply ingrained in decision-making processes, resulting in a lack of diversity at senior levels.

2. Tokenism and Lack of Meaningful Change

In some Indian organizations, DEI initiatives have been implemented for show rather than being driven by a genuine commitment to creating an inclusive environment. Tokenism—where a few employees from underrepresented groups are included for appearances but are not meaningfully integrated into decision-making or leadership processes—has been a significant challenge in many companies. Tokenistic efforts can lead to resentment among diverse employees, as they may feel that their inclusion is more about fulfilling quotas than about their value or contributions.

For instance, some organizations may celebrate "Diversity Day" or introduce diversity training sessions without taking tangible actions to address systemic issues or make substantial changes to workplace culture. Without a robust action plan and sustained leadership support, such efforts may not lead to lasting change.

3. Cultural Resistance to Change

Many Indian companies, particularly those with deeply rooted traditional practices and hierarchical structures, face significant cultural resistance when it comes to implementing DEI initiatives. Employees may resist the idea of change, especially when they perceive it as threatening to the existing power structures. Senior leaders, especially in conservative sectors, may not always be open to the idea of promoting diversity and inclusion, as it challenges traditional norms and practices.

This resistance often manifests in employees being unwilling to engage in conversations about diversity or inclusion, reluctance to support policies that promote gender equality or caste equity, and even pushback against initiatives like affirmative action or pay equity programs.

4. Ineffective or Inadequate Training

A lack of proper training and education on DEI issues has been a common failure in many Indian organizations. Diversity and inclusion training programs may be superficial or insufficiently focused on creating lasting behavioral changes. Many companies only offer one-time training sessions without providing ongoing education and support for employees and managers. Without continuous reinforcement and the creation of spaces for open discussions, DEI initiatives are unlikely to lead to meaningful cultural shifts.

5. Limited Representation at Leadership Levels

Against making strides in diverse hiring practices, many organizations still struggle with the lack of diverse representation in leadership and decision-making roles. Indian organizations often have leadership teams that are homogeneous in terms of gender, caste, and regional background. This lack of diverse representation at the top levels not only affects the success of DEI initiatives but also limits the organization's ability to fully understand and address the challenges faced by employees from marginalized groups.

6. Insufficient Data and Accountability Mechanisms

Many companies fail to track and measure the success of their DEI programs. Without robust data on hiring practices, promotions, employee turnover, and satisfaction, organizations cannot accurately assess the effectiveness of their DEI initiatives. Without clear accountability mechanisms and regular assessments, organizations may not be able to identify gaps or areas of improvement in their DEI efforts. For instance, organizations may not have systems in place to track pay equity, diversity in leadership, or the overall inclusivity of their work culture.

Measuring DEI Success

To measure the success of DEI initiatives, organizations need to track both qualitative and quantitative metrics. Common metrics include the representation of diverse groups in the workforce, employee engagement and satisfaction surveys, pay equity audits, retention rates, and the inclusion of diverse perspectives in leadership roles. For instance, companies like Tata Consultancy Services (TCS) and Wipro measure their DEI progress by assessing gender diversity, employee engagement, and the success of employee resource groups.

Excluding to tracking these metrics, it's important for organizations to ensure that DEI is woven into the fabric of their corporate strategies, with leadership being accountable for promoting diversity, equity, and inclusion across all levels.

Measuring the success of Diversity, Equity, and Inclusion (DEI) initiatives is crucial for organizations to assess the effectiveness of their efforts and identify areas for improvement. In contempt of that, measuring DEI success can be challenging, as it involves both quantitative and qualitative aspects, and requires tracking both short-term and long-term outcomes. Indian organizations, like those globally, are increasingly recognizing the importance of integrating DEI into their corporate strategies and using various metrics to gauge their success.

One of the most common methods to measure DEI success is through demographic data. This involves analyzing the diversity of the workforce, specifically in terms of gender, caste, religion, disability status, and other dimensions of diversity. Tracking the representation of diverse groups at various organizational levels, including leadership roles, is an essential step in determining how well the organization is advancing its DEI goals. For example, companies like Tata Consultancy Services (TCS) and Infosys track the gender ratio in their workforce, setting targets to increase the representation of women in leadership positions and technical roles.

Also, recruitment metrics are another valuable indicator of DEI success. By examining the composition of candidates applying for jobs, being shortlisted, and hired, organizations can assess whether they are attracting a diverse pool of applicants. If certain groups are underrepresented in applications or hiring, it may indicate a need to revisit the organization's recruitment strategies or identify any biases in the hiring process. Leading Indian companies such as Flipkart and Mahindra & Mahindra focus on diversifying their talent pools by using AI-driven recruitment tools to eliminate unconscious biases and ensure equal opportunity for all candidates.

Auxiliary important metric in measuring DEI success is employee engagement and satisfaction. Employee surveys, focus groups, and feedback mechanisms can help determine how inclusive and equitable employees perceive the workplace environment to be. Regularly measuring employee satisfaction in relation to DEI can highlight areas where the organization may need to improve, such as addressing microaggressions, improving work-life balance, or fostering a culture of inclusivity. For instance, Wipro conducts regular surveys to assess employee satisfaction and engagement, with a specific focus on DEI-related concerns.

Retention rates are also a key metric in evaluating DEI success. A high turnover rate among underrepresented groups can indicate that employees do not feel supported, valued, or included within the organization. Organizations must track the retention of employees from diverse backgrounds to ensure that their DEI efforts are not only attracting diverse talent but also retaining them in the long term. Companies such as Accenture India have made efforts to reduce attrition among women by introducing flexible work policies and creating a more inclusive work environment.

Equity in career progression and compensation is another important area to measure. DEI success is not only about having a diverse workforce but also ensuring that all employees have equal opportunities for growth, advancement, and compensation. Regular pay audits, performance reviews, and career progression data can provide insights into whether employees from all backgrounds are being treated equitably in terms of promotions, raises, and developmental opportunities. For instance, Indian companies like Zensar Technologies conduct pay audits and analyze performance reviews to ensure that employees are evaluated fairly, regardless of their gender, caste, or background.

16. SUSTAINABILITY PRACTICES AND EMPLOYEE ADVOCACY

In India, sustainability has gained significant attention in recent years. Indian companies, including Tata Group, Wipro, and Infosys, have integrated sustainability into their core business strategies, often aligning their practices with the global sustainability goals. Indian firms are also adopting various measures such as sustainable sourcing, waste management, water conservation, and renewable energy investments. As highlighted by Agarwal (2018), "Indian companies are increasingly incorporating sustainability as a central part of their strategy due to growing environmental concerns and consumer demand for sustainable practices."

Agarwal, R. (2018). *Corporate Sustainability Practices in India: An Overview.* International Journal of Business and Management Studies, 8(1), 12-25.

Sustainability Practices and Employee Advocacy in Indian Organizations

Sustainability has become a key focus for organizations worldwide, including in India, as businesses recognize the importance of balancing economic, environmental, and social considerations in their operations. As more companies adopt sustainability practices, there is growing recognition that employees play a pivotal role in driving sustainability goals forward. Employee advocacy, which involves employees actively supporting and promoting their organization's sustainability initiatives, is a powerful tool for enhancing organizational impact and fostering a culture of responsibility.

Sustainability practices and employee advocacy are integral to creating an organizational culture that values long-term responsibility and growth. In India, where sustainability challenges are both local and global, companies like Infosys, Wipro, and Tata Group have set benchmarks in adopting environmental and social practices while involving their employees in these efforts. By aligning employee engagement with sustainability goals and fostering a culture of responsibility, Indian organizations can build a more sustainable future for both their business and society. Although, for these efforts to be truly successful, companies must overcome challenges related to awareness, engagement, and resource allocation, ensuring that sustainability becomes deeply embedded in both organizational practices and employee behavior.

Role of Employees in Sustainability

Employees are central to any organization's sustainability journey. The involvement of employees goes beyond passive awareness to active participation, where they become advocates for the company's sustainability objectives. This shift from a top-down approach to a more inclusive and participatory model can significantly enhance the effectiveness of sustainability efforts.

When employees are engaged with sustainability practices, they are more likely to champion these initiatives, share their benefits with others, and contribute creatively to finding new solutions to sustainability challenges. As sustainability becomes an integrated part of organizational culture, employees can act as the driving force, bringing innovative ideas, encouraging peer participation, and creating a more sustainable work environment.

For example, **Infosys**, a leader in India's IT sector, has adopted a comprehensive sustainability strategy that not only focuses on reducing carbon emissions and waste but also encourages employees to be part of sustainability efforts. Through initiatives such as **Infosys Green Teams**, employees actively participate in the company's sustainability programs, from tree-planting campaigns to energy conservation projects, making them feel directly involved in the organization's sustainability efforts.

Similarly, **Wipro**, a multinational IT company, has consistently embedded sustainability into its core operations, and its employees are encouraged to act as sustainability ambassadors. Wipro's **Sustainability Champions** program allows employees to engage in environmental and social initiatives, such as promoting energy-efficient practices and reducing plastic use, thus fostering a culture where sustainability is seen as a shared responsibility.

The Way Forward

To ensure that sustainability practices are deeply embedded in the culture of Indian organizations, companies must move beyond implementing one-off projects and instead integrate sustainability into every aspect of their operations. Employee advocacy is key to achieving this integration, as employees are the ones who will help drive these initiatives forward.

By aligning their sustainability goals with employee engagement, providing regular training and resources, and recognizing employees for their contributions to sustainability, organizations can create a culture where sustainability is not just a corporate goal but a shared responsibility. Indian companies like **Infosys**, **Wipro**, **Tata Group**, and **Accenture** are setting important precedents, but broader efforts to embed sustainability in the corporate DNA will require overcoming the challenges of awareness, resource allocation, and resistance to change.

Through these collective efforts, Indian organizations can not only drive sustainability goals but also create lasting positive change for their employees, communities, and the environment. By fostering a culture of advocacy, responsibility, and engagement, they can help ensure that sustainability becomes a fundamental part of the business model for the future.

Sustainability Practices in Indian Organizations

Sustainability in Indian organizations has evolved significantly over the past decade, with many companies adopting policies and practices aimed at reducing their environmental footprint, supporting social causes, and promoting long-term economic viability. Sustainability in the Indian corporate context encompasses various dimensions, such as energy efficiency, waste management, water conservation, and responsible sourcing, as well as broader social initiatives related to community development and employee well-being.

1. Environmental Sustainability

Indian organizations, particularly in sectors such as manufacturing, energy, and retail, are increasingly focused on adopting eco-friendly practices. Companies like **Tata Group**, **Infosys**, and **Wipro** have led the way in environmental sustainability by reducing their carbon emissions, adopting renewable energy solutions, and focusing on sustainable resource management.

For instance, **Infosys** has made significant investments in green buildings, with its campuses powered by solar energy and water recycling systems. The company has also set ambitious goals to achieve carbon neutrality and reduce water usage, making it one of the leaders in sustainability within the Indian tech industry. Similarly, **Tata Motors** has focused on reducing emissions through the development of electric vehicles (EVs), aligning with India's broader push toward green energy and reducing dependency on fossil fuels.

2. Social Sustainability

Beyond environmental sustainability, Indian organizations are also addressing social sustainability, which includes efforts to improve employee welfare, community engagement, and social equity. **Hindustan Unilever**, for example, has implemented several initiatives to support women's empowerment, enhance the livelihoods of rural communities, and improve health and hygiene in underserved areas. **Mahindra & Mahindra** has taken a strong stance on social sustainability by promoting inclusive growth through initiatives that support farmers, rural populations, and education in underdeveloped regions.

3. Sustainable Supply Chain Management

Sustainability in the supply chain is another growing focus area for Indian organizations. Companies are increasingly focusing on ensuring that their suppliers meet environmental and social standards, and they are working to eliminate wasteful practices. **Wipro** has adopted a green supply chain strategy that includes evaluating suppliers based on their sustainability practices and encouraging them to adopt energy-efficient processes.

4. Sustainable Employee Practices

Many organizations in India have also implemented employee-specific sustainability programs, such as promoting work-life balance, providing health and wellness benefits, and offering flexible working arrangements. Companies are increasingly aware that employee well-being and engagement are integral to overall organizational sustainability, and have taken steps to integrate these values into their workplace culture.

Employee Advocacy in Sustainability

Employee advocacy refers to the active involvement of employees in promoting and supporting the company's goals, policies, and practices, both internally and externally. When it comes to sustainability, employees can act as ambassadors for the organization's sustainability initiatives by spreading awareness, advocating for environmental and social responsibility, and helping to integrate sustainable practices into daily operations.

1. Employee Engagement in Sustainability Initiatives

For sustainability practices to be successful, it is critical that employees are not only aware of the company's initiatives but are also engaged in them. Employee advocacy in sustainability starts with fostering a sense of ownership and responsibility toward sustainability goals within the organization. When employees feel personally connected to sustainability efforts, they are more likely to advocate for the company's green initiatives and participate actively in them.

Indian companies like **Tata Consultancy Services (TCS)** have taken proactive steps to involve employees in sustainability efforts. TCS encourages employees to engage in activities such as volunteering for environmental cleanup programs, participating in tree plantation drives, and advocating for energy-efficient office practices. By providing employees with the tools, resources, and platforms to advocate for sustainability, companies are able to turn their workforce into active promoters of sustainability.

2. Internal Communication and Advocacy Platforms

Effective internal communication plays a crucial role in employee advocacy for sustainability. Companies like **Wipro** and **Accenture India** have implemented communication platforms that keep employees informed about the latest sustainability goals, achievements, and opportunities to contribute. These platforms allow employees to discuss ideas, raise concerns, and collaborate on sustainability initiatives, fostering a sense of shared responsibility and purpose.

In some companies, employees who are passionate about sustainability may be appointed as **"Green Ambassadors"** or **"Sustainability Champions,"** responsible for promoting green initiatives across departments. This type of employee advocacy helps generate enthusiasm and buy-in for sustainability programs, ensuring that sustainability is embedded into every level of the organization.

3. Employee-Led Sustainability Initiatives

Employee-led sustainability initiatives are one of the most effective ways to foster a culture of sustainability within an organization. Employees, especially younger generations, are increasingly motivated by environmental and social causes and are more likely to push for changes that align with these values. Organizations that encourage employees to lead sustainability initiatives often see greater buy-in and participation in these programs.

For example, at **Infosys**, employees have initiated several grassroots sustainability programs, including waste reduction campaigns, awareness drives on reducing plastic consumption, and advocating for sustainable commuting practices. The organization has not only supported these initiatives but has also allowed employees to take ownership of them, further reinforcing the importance of employee advocacy in achieving sustainability goals.

4. Incentives for Employee Advocacy

To drive greater involvement, many organizations have introduced incentive programs to reward employees who contribute to sustainability efforts. These can include recognition through awards, career development opportunities, or even financial incentives. By acknowledging and rewarding employees for their role in advancing sustainability practices, organizations can further motivate employees to act as advocates for sustainability.

At **Cognizant**, for example, employees who actively contribute to environmental initiatives or community-based sustainability projects are recognized during company-wide meetings and are often given leadership opportunities in sustainability-related programs. This recognition not only boosts employee morale but also highlights the company's commitment to sustainability.

Challenges in Employee Advocacy for Sustainability

While employee advocacy can be a powerful tool for promoting sustainability, there are several challenges that organizations may face in this area:

1. **Lack of Awareness and Education**: Employees may not always fully understand the significance of sustainability initiatives or how they can contribute to them. This lack of awareness can limit employee participation and advocacy efforts. It is crucial for organizations to invest in continuous education and training on sustainability practices.

2. **Misalignment with Organizational Goals**: In some cases, employees may not feel that their personal values align

with the company's sustainability goals. This can lead to disengagement or skepticism about the effectiveness of sustainability programs. Organizations must ensure that their sustainability objectives are clearly communicated and aligned with the values of their workforce.

3. **Resistance to Change**: Resistance to change is a common challenge in many organizations, especially when implementing new sustainability practices that may require employees to change their daily routines or habits. Overcoming resistance requires strong leadership, effective communication, and a clear rationale for why sustainability is important.

4. **Inadequate Support for Employee-Led Initiatives**: While employee-led initiatives can be highly effective, they may lack the necessary resources and support to thrive. Organizations must ensure that they provide the tools, time, and recognition needed for employees to successfully advocate for sustainability.

Sustainability practices and employee advocacy are inextricably linked in today's business landscape. Indian organizations that embrace sustainability initiatives and encourage employee involvement in these efforts are more likely to create a culture of sustainability that benefits both the environment and the organization. Companies like Infosys, Wipro, and Tata Group have set the benchmark for successful integration of sustainability into business practices, with active employee advocacy playing a crucial role in driving these initiatives. In contempt of that, challenges remain in terms of employee engagement, awareness, and overcoming resistance to change. By addressing these challenges, organizations can leverage employee advocacy to amplify the impact of their sustainability practices and create a lasting culture of responsibility and innovation.

17. THE GIG ECONOMY AND REMOTE WORK

The gig economy refers to a labor market characterized by the prevalence of short-term, flexible jobs or freelance work, where individuals are hired to perform specific tasks or projects for businesses or clients. In this economy, workers typically have the autonomy to choose when and where they work, often through digital platforms that connect them to these opportunities. It contrasts with traditional employment models, where employees typically have permanent, full-time roles with benefits.

Kalleberg, A. L., & Dunn, M. (2016). *Good Jobs, Bad Jobs in the Gig Economy.* Economic Policy Institute.

The Future of the Gig Economy and Remote Work in India

The gig economy and remote work are expected to continue growing in India, driven by advances in technology, changing employee expectations, and evolving business models. To thrive in this new work environment, Indian organizations must adopt flexible, inclusive, and adaptive policies that cater to both gig workers and remote employees.

HR professionals will play a crucial role in managing the challenges of these work models, from creating effective performance management systems to fostering a culture of inclusion and engagement. As more organizations embrace the gig economy and remote work, the future of work in India will be characterized by greater flexibility, greater autonomy for employees, and more diverse opportunities for businesses to tap into talent from across the globe.

Ultimately, organizations that successfully navigate these trends will be better positioned to innovate, stay competitive, and build a more resilient and agile workforce in the face of future challenges.

The future of the gig economy and remote work in India is shaping up to be a crucial aspect of the country's rapidly evolving work culture. As businesses and workers continue to embrace flexibility, new models and practices will emerge, and it is essential for management students, HR, and OB professionals to understand these shifts. The key trends expected to drive this evolution include hybrid models, increased digitalization, employee well-being, and the development of regulatory frameworks.

As remote work and the gig economy continue to gain momentum, hybrid work models are anticipated to become the norm for many Indian organizations. A hybrid work model allows employees to have the flexibility to choose between working remotely, in a hybrid setup, or on-site depending on their job roles, personal preferences, and the needs of the business. In sectors such as technology, consulting, and customer service, this flexibility has proven to be an attractive proposition for both employees and employers. Companies like Tata Consultancy Services (TCS), Wipro, and Infosys have already adopted such hybrid models, giving employees the option to work from home a few days a week while still maintaining in-office interactions for collaborative purposes. The introduction of hybrid models is expected to enhance work-life balance, reduce employee turnover, and provide businesses with a competitive edge in attracting top talent. For management students and HR professionals, this trend will require the development of new policies and systems to ensure that employees feel equally engaged and supported, whether they are working remotely or from the office.

Alongside hybrid work, digitalization will play an even more central role in connecting businesses with talent and managing operations in the future. The rise of the gig economy, where workers are hired on short-term contracts or project-based work, and the growing adoption of remote work, means that organizations will increasingly rely on digital platforms and tools. These technologies will be essential for streamlining processes such as project management, collaboration, and performance tracking. Platforms such as **Slack, Zoom, Microsoft Teams**, and **Trello** will continue to support teams in staying connected and productive, regardless of where they are located. Also, cloud-based systems and AI-driven tools will become more integral to day-to-day operations. For instance, recruitment platforms like **Upwork** or **Freelancer.com** are already connecting Indian workers with international opportunities, and similar tools are likely to become more widespread. HR and OB professionals in Indian organizations must understand how to effectively integrate these tools, ensuring smooth operations and maintaining team cohesion, even when employees are working remotely or on a project basis.

Employee well-being will become an increasingly important focus for organizations as remote work and gig work become more common. Workers in both of these setups face unique challenges, such as isolation, burnout, and a lack of personal connection with colleagues. As employees in remote and gig roles often miss the social interaction that comes with working in an office environment, companies will need to prioritize the mental health and well-being of their workforce. This can include offering resources like mental health support services, flexible working hours to promote work-life balance, and providing opportunities for virtual team-building and networking. Indian organizations will need to go beyond just offering physical wellness programs to create a more holistic approach that nurtures emotional and psychological well-being. Companies like **Wipro** and **Accenture** are already incorporating well-being programs into their employee engagement strategies, and this trend is expected to grow as organizations recognize the long-term benefits of a healthy, happy workforce. For HR professionals, this will require new training and resources to help employees manage the challenges of working remotely or as part of the gig economy.

The future of the gig economy in India also raises important questions about regulation and legal protections for gig workers. In India, where a significant portion of the workforce is engaged in gig or freelance work, there is often a lack of formal labor rights for these employees. Unlike full-time employees, gig workers may not have access to healthcare, paid leave, job security, or other benefits that are typically provided by employers. This creates a situation where gig workers may face financial insecurity or lack support when dealing with illness, personal crises, or career growth challenges. Even with that, the Indian government has started taking steps to address these issues. Recent discussions around creating a **Social Security Code** for gig workers have shown promise in providing legal recognition and protections, including access to health benefits and other welfare measures. Indian companies, particularly those in the gig economy, will need to adapt to these changes and ensure they comply with new regulations that protect gig workers. For HR and management professionals, this will mean understanding the evolving regulatory landscape and ensuring that their organizations offer fair compensation and benefits to gig workers, while also providing the legal safeguards required by law.

The Shift to Remote Work

The COVID-19 pandemic played a pivotal role in the widespread adoption of remote work in India. Before the pandemic, remote work was limited to specific industries like IT and some startups. while, the pandemic forced a sudden transition, and many organizations across various sectors, including education, customer support, and finance, embraced remote work to maintain business continuity.

In India, remote work offers employees greater flexibility, eliminating long commutes and providing a better work-life balance. A 2023 survey by **LinkedIn** highlighted that over 60% of Indian employees preferred flexible work arrangements. This is why many employees in knowledge-based industries, such as IT, software development, marketing, and consulting, find remote work to be a more productive and less distracting environment compared to traditional office settings.

Remote work has also opened up opportunities for organizations to tap into talent pools beyond metro cities. Previously, many companies were limited to hiring talent from tier-1 cities like Bengaluru, Mumbai, and Delhi. Still, with remote work, organizations can now access talent from smaller towns and cities across India, broadening their hiring horizons and reducing the skills gap in underrepresented regions.

Remote work has allowed Indian companies to tap into a wider talent pool, enabling them to hire employees from various parts of the country, including tier-2 and tier-3 cities. This geographical flexibility helps organizations overcome the challenges of talent shortages in major metropolitan areas and attract diverse skill sets from all corners of the country. Companies like **Tata Consultancy Services (TCS)** and **Infosys** have embraced remote work to not only retain their current workforce but also reduce office space costs.

Nevertheless, remote work also presents challenges related to employee engagement, collaboration, and maintaining a cohesive organizational culture. Many organizations have found it difficult to replicate the same level of interaction and communication that occurs in a physical office environment. Leaders and HR professionals need to invest in tools and technologies that enable remote teams to stay connected and productive. Platforms like **Slack, Zoom,** and **Microsoft Teams** have become essential for communication and collaboration in remote teams.

Too, remote work can create a sense of isolation among employees, which may impact their mental health and overall well-being. Companies must take proactive measures to address these concerns by providing mental health support, promoting work-life balance, and encouraging social interactions through virtual team-building activities.

Benefits of the Gig Economy and Remote Work

1. **Flexibility and Agility:** Both the gig economy and remote work offer flexibility to both organizations and employees. Businesses can hire workers as needed, scaling up or down depending on demand. Employees, in turn, can choose work arrangements that best fit their lifestyle, such as working from home or choosing short-term assignments that align with their interests and skills.

2. **Cost Savings:** Organizations in India can save on operational costs such as office space, utilities, and infrastructure by adopting remote work practices. Similarly, by hiring gig workers on a contract basis, businesses can reduce costs associated with full-time employment, such as healthcare benefits and pension plans.

3. **Access to a Global Talent Pool:** Remote work allows organizations to tap into a global talent pool, which can be especially beneficial for companies in the IT and tech sectors. The gig economy also enables Indian professionals to connect with clients worldwide,

expanding their market reach and creating opportunities for skill development.

4. **Increased Productivity:** Studies have shown that remote workers often experience higher productivity levels due to fewer distractions, the flexibility to create their own work environment, and the ability to manage their time effectively. This is particularly true for Indian employees in knowledge-based industries like IT and consulting, where task-focused work can be done efficiently from home.

Challenges of the Gig Economy and Remote Work

Employee Engagement and Retention: One of the biggest challenges in both the gig economy and remote work models is maintaining employee engagement and ensuring long-term retention. Gig workers may lack the same sense of belonging and commitment to the organization as full-time employees, which can lead to high turnover. Remote workers may also feel disconnected from their teams and miss the social interaction and camaraderie of an office environment.

Performance Management: Managing the performance of gig workers and remote employees can be challenging, as traditional methods of evaluation may not be effective in these models. Managers must adapt their approach, using clear goal-setting, regular check-ins, and performance metrics to ensure that employees meet expectations. This requires a shift in management style, with a focus on output and results rather than process and time spent.

Security and Confidentiality: Remote work, particularly in sectors like IT and finance, raises concerns about data security and confidentiality. Organizations must invest in secure communication channels, collaboration tools, and cybersecurity measures to protect sensitive information when employees are working from home or from various locations.

Legal and Regulatory Compliance: The gig economy poses challenges for organizations in terms of ensuring compliance with labor laws and protecting the rights of workers. In India, gig workers are often not covered under the same labor protections as full-time employees, which can lead to exploitation or a lack of job security. Organizations must navigate these complexities to ensure fair treatment of all workers and avoid legal pitfalls.

18. THE CHANGE CURVE AND EMPLOYEE ADAPTABILITY

The Change Curve is a model that describes the emotional and psychological responses individuals experience when undergoing change. It suggests that people typically go through a series of stages as they adapt to new situations, including stages like shock, denial, frustration, depression, experimentation, and acceptance. This model is often used in change management to help organizations support employees as they transition through these stages of change.

Kubler-Ross, E. (1969). *On Death and Dying*. Macmillan.

The Change Curve and Employee Adaptability refer to the process through which employees adjust to organizational change, highlighting the emotional and behavioral shifts that occur as individuals move from initial resistance to acceptance and commitment. Understanding the Change Curve and fostering employee adaptability are critical for HR and OB professionals, as these elements directly influence how smoothly and successfully an organization can implement change initiatives.

The Change Curve is a model that illustrates the stages individuals typically experience when confronted with change. Initially developed by Elisabeth Kübler-Ross to explain the emotional responses of individuals facing terminal illness, the model was later adapted to the workplace to describe how employees react to change. It consists of several stages, including denial, anger, bargaining, depression, and finally acceptance or integration. However, it's important to note that not all employees will experience every stage, nor will they experience them in the same way or in a linear progression.

In the context of Indian organizations, where change can be particularly challenging due to deeply ingrained cultural practices, hierarchical structures, and sometimes a resistance to new ways of doing things, the Change Curve becomes a valuable framework for understanding and managing employee reactions. For example, when a company like **Tata Steel** or **Reliance Industries** introduces a new technology or restructuring initiative, employees may initially react with resistance or fear, especially if the change threatens their roles or routines. This stage, often marked by denial or anger, can be seen in Indian organizations where job security and stability are valued.

For HR and OB professionals, understanding the Change Curve and employee adaptability is key to managing organizational change. The goal is to help employees move through the stages of the curve effectively, minimizing disruption and fostering a smooth transition. To facilitate this, HR professionals need to provide clear and consistent communication, create training programs, and offer emotional and practical support. Effective leadership plays a crucial role in guiding employees through these transitions, ensuring that they feel heard, supported, and involved in the change process.

The role of employee adaptability is essential in this context. Adaptability refers to an employee's ability to adjust their thinking, behavior, and actions in response to new conditions, challenges, and environments. In India, where rapid changes in technology, business models, and market conditions are increasingly common, organizations need employees who are flexible, resilient, and capable of embracing new ideas and methods.

Employees who are adaptable are more likely to exhibit positive behaviors such as problem-solving, open communication, and a willingness to learn new skills. Companies like **Infosys** and **Wipro** have recognized the importance of adaptability and have implemented learning and development initiatives to nurture this quality among their workforce. Providing employees with opportunities to upskill or reskill ensures they remain relevant and confident when facing changes, whether related to new technologies, work structures, or business strategies.

One way to support adaptability is through creating a culture of continuous learning. Indian organizations can encourage employees to develop a growth mindset—believing that their abilities can be developed through dedication and hard work. This mindset helps employees view change not as a threat but as an opportunity for personal and professional growth. By promoting adaptability through training programs, leadership development, and supportive mentoring, organizations can build a workforce that is more resilient and better equipped to navigate change.

In analysing fact, understanding the Change Curve and fostering employee adaptability are essential components for managing organizational change effectively. HR and OB professionals in Indian organizations need to ensure that employees are supported through the emotional and practical challenges of change. By investing in communication, training, and leadership, organizations can help employees transition smoothly through the stages of the Change Curve, ultimately enabling them to embrace change and thrive in new and evolving business environments.

The Change Curve is a psychological model that illustrates the emotional stages people typically experience when faced with change. Originally developed by Elisabeth Kübler-Ross in 1969 to describe the emotional responses of individuals diagnosed with terminal illnesses, the model was later adapted to organizational change. The concept has become highly relevant in the fields of Human Resources (HR) and Organizational Behavior (OB), particularly when managing transitions like mergers, restructures, leadership changes, or technological upgrades within companies.

The Change Curve is often visualized as a graph with emotional responses plotted on the vertical axis and the passage of time or change events on the horizontal axis. As employees experience change, they usually go through a series of emotional states. These stages commonly include initial denial, followed by resistance, exploration, and eventually acceptance. It's important to note that not everyone progresses through these stages in the same way, nor do they experience them in a linear fashion. Some may skip certain stages entirely, while others may linger in one for an extended period.

In Indian workplaces, employees' reactions to change may also be influenced by societal and cultural factors, such as respect for authority and seniority. Changes that come from top-down decisions may be met with skepticism or resistance, as many employees might prefer stability and fear the unknown. This highlights the importance of addressing the emotional aspects of change in Indian organizations, where the perception of power and authority is often more rigid. Managers must recognize these emotional responses and work to address them through communication, support, and empathy.

For HR and OB professionals, applying the Change Curve in India means recognizing the various stages employees go through and being prepared to guide them effectively through each one. For instance, when employees first hear about a change, they may enter the denial phase, refusing to accept the need for change or doubting its necessity. As change is implemented, they might enter the resistance phase, where they express frustration, confusion, or even anger about how it will impact them personally. In such situations, HR professionals should engage in open communication, explain the rationale behind the change, and provide support and training to ease the transition.

As employees move forward, they may begin to explore new ways of working or adapting to the change. This exploration phase is when they start to realize that the change might offer new opportunities or improvements, such as enhanced efficiency or career growth. HR professionals in Indian organizations can support this phase by offering coaching, mentoring, and peer support systems to help employees adapt and thrive.

In the context of Indian organizational behavior, the Change Curve aligns with key principles like employee motivation, leadership, and communication. It underscores the importance of managing employees' emotional responses and ensuring that they are emotionally and intellectually prepared for change. The model is also particularly useful in addressing employee concerns in organizations where the hierarchical system often means changes are imposed from the top down. In such settings, providing regular updates, soliciting feedback, and involving employees in the change process can go a long way in ensuring smoother transitions.

---

19. MENTAL HEALTH INITIATIVES IN MODERN WORKPLACES

Mental Health refers to a person's emotional, psychological, and social well-being. It affects how individuals think, feel, and act in their daily lives. Mental health also influences how people handle stress, relate to others, and make choices. It is essential at every stage of life, from childhood through adulthood. Mental health problems can arise due to various factors, including biological, psychological, and environmental influences. In workplaces, promoting mental health is crucial for ensuring employee well-being, productivity, and overall organizational success.

World Health Organization (WHO). (2004). *Promoting Mental Health: Concepts, Emerging Evidence, Practice.* WHO.

Mental health initiatives in modern workplaces are becoming increasingly important as organizations recognize the significant impact of employee well-being on productivity, engagement, and overall organizational success. Mental health issues such as stress, anxiety, depression, and burnout can hinder an employee's ability to perform at their best, leading to absenteeism, lower job satisfaction, and higher turnover rates. As a result, businesses are now adopting strategies and programs to support the mental health of their employees and create a supportive work environment.

In the context of Indian organizations, mental health initiatives have gained traction in recent years, especially following the COVID-19 pandemic, which brought mental health challenges to the forefront. The pandemic, with its uncertainties and remote work dynamics, triggered a surge in stress-related disorders. As businesses shifted to hybrid or remote work, employees experienced feelings of isolation, burnout, and heightened stress due to blurred work-life boundaries. Indian companies, recognizing the importance of employee well-being, are increasingly offering mental health resources, services, and programs to help their workforce cope with these challenges.

The first and most crucial step that organizations can take to promote mental health is to foster a culture of openness. In Indian workplaces, mental health has commonly been a taboo subject. Many employees feel uncomfortable discussing their mental health struggles due to fear of stigma or negative career implications. By creating a culture where mental health is openly discussed, organizations can reduce stigma and encourage employees to seek help when needed. This can be achieved by training managers to recognize signs of mental health issues and to offer support without judgment.

Companies like **Infosys**, **Tata Consultancy Services (TCS)**, and **Wipro** have begun integrating mental health programs as part of their employee welfare initiatives. These companies are offering Employee Assistance Programs (EAPs) that provide confidential counselling and support services to employees. Over and above, many organizations are introducing wellness programs that include meditation, yoga, and mindfulness activities to help employees manage stress and improve their emotional resilience.

Technology has also played a key role in promoting mental health at work. Digital platforms and mobile applications now provide employees with access to mental health resources at their fingertips. For instance, apps that provide meditation exercises, virtual therapy sessions, and self-care tips are becoming popular in workplaces. Companies like **Zoho** and **Flipkart** have also incorporated these digital solutions into their employee wellness programs to enhance accessibility and ensure that employees can seek help discreetly and conveniently.

Flexible work arrangements, which have become a norm in many Indian organizations, also contribute to reducing stress and improving mental health. Allowing employees to work from home, adopt hybrid work models, or implement flexible hours can help employees achieve a better work-life balance and reduce stress levels. This is particularly significant in India, where long working hours and commute times can add to the burden of employees. In companies where remote work is the norm, offering flexibility in work schedules can help employees manage their workload more effectively while also attending to personal needs and commitments.

For this reason, management training on mental health is crucial for addressing mental health challenges at the workplace. HR professionals and leaders must be equipped with the knowledge and skills to identify when an employee is struggling and how to offer appropriate support. Training leaders to understand the psychological pressures their teams may be facing and offering guidance on how to manage workloads effectively can reduce workplace stress. Indian organizations are increasingly integrating such training into their leadership development programs, ensuring that managers are better prepared to address mental health concerns proactively.

Support for employees with mental health challenges also includes creating a supportive work environment where team members encourage one another and where managers regularly check in with their teams. Encouragement and active listening can go a long way in fostering an emotionally supportive workplace. This is especially important in India, where high job expectations and societal pressures often contribute to stress and mental health issues.

Also, Indian companies are focusing on the long-term impact of mental health by implementing initiatives that promote resilience, emotional intelligence, and psychological safety. These programs aim to equip employees with tools to better manage stress, foster healthy relationships at work, and encourage open communication. By incorporating mental health into the overall organizational culture, businesses not only enhance employee well-being but also improve retention, engagement, and productivity.

In simple words, mental health initiatives in modern workplaces are essential for the well-being of employees and the long-term success of organizations. In Indian companies, these initiatives are increasingly becoming an integral part of

HR and organizational behaviour strategies. By offering counselling services, promoting a supportive and open culture, leveraging technology, and providing flexible work arrangements, Indian organizations can create a workplace where employees feel valued, supported, and empowered to manage their mental health. By focusing on mental health, businesses can improve employee engagement, reduce turnover, and enhance overall productivity, leading to a more resilient and sustainable workforce.

Mental health strategies implemented by Indian companies have become increasingly important as organizations recognize the vital role employee well-being plays in overall productivity and engagement. These strategies are particularly relevant for HR and Organizational Behavior (OB) professionals, as they are responsible for creating work environments that promote not only physical health but also mental health. Below are some of the mental health strategies adopted by Indian companies that HR and OB professionals can implement, which may also serve as valuable insights for management students:

1. Employee Assistance Programs (EAPs)

Many Indian companies, such as **Infosys**, **Tata Consultancy Services (TCS)**, and **Wipro**, have integrated Employee Assistance Programs into their overall HR strategy. These programs provide employees with confidential counseling services to help them manage personal or work-related issues. EAPs may include professional counseling, stress management workshops, and support for substance abuse or family issues. For HR professionals and students, implementing or recommending EAPs in organizational settings can significantly enhance employee well-being.

Implementation Insight for HR Professionals: Establish a third-party service provider to ensure confidentiality, and create awareness about the availability of these services to reduce stigma. Managers can also be trained to refer employees to these services when necessary.

2. Mental Health Awareness and Training

Organizations like **Wipro** and **Accenture** have introduced mental health awareness campaigns to educate employees and leadership about mental health challenges, the signs of mental distress, and how to offer support. This helps to reduce stigma and encourages employees to seek help when needed.

Implementation Insight for HR Professionals: Organize workshops and training for managers and employees on recognizing mental health issues, stress management techniques, and how to engage in open conversations about mental health. This can be incorporated into onboarding processes and leadership training programs for long-term impact.

3. Flexible Work Arrangements

In India, organizations like **Flipkart**, **Zoho**, and **Dell** have adopted flexible work policies to reduce stress and improve work-life balance. This includes options for working from home, flexible hours, and hybrid work models. During the pandemic, remote work became particularly vital for maintaining employee mental health by reducing stressors such as long commute times, lack of family time, and workplace pressure.

Implementation Insight for HR Professionals: Implement flexible work hours or hybrid models where employees can choose between in-office and remote work based on personal preferences. Create clear guidelines around flexible work policies to ensure consistency and transparency.

4. Workplace Wellness Programs

Workplace wellness programs are an effective strategy for promoting both physical and mental well-being. Indian organizations such as **Mindtree** and **L&T** have incorporated wellness initiatives, including regular meditation and yoga sessions, mindfulness workshops, and physical fitness challenges. These programs help employees manage stress, build resilience, and improve overall mental health.

Implementation Insight for OB and HR Professionals: Promote initiatives like yoga, meditation, or mindfulness-based stress reduction (MBSR) programs as part of the corporate wellness offerings. Encourage regular breaks during work hours to engage in these activities and support employees' well-being holistically.

5. Supportive and Open Work Culture

Companies like **Mahindra & Mahindra** have fostered an inclusive and open workplace culture where employees feel comfortable discussing their mental health struggles. These companies encourage peer support, active listening, and regular feedback channels to address any concerns regarding mental health in a constructive manner.

Implementation Insight for HR Professionals: Cultivate a work environment where employees feel safe to share their mental health challenges without fear of judgment. Create open lines of communication with HR or leadership to address mental health concerns proactively and ensure that employees have access to the support they need.

6. Digital Mental Health Tools and Resources

In light of the digital transformation, organizations like **HCL Technologies** and **Zoho** have turned to digital platforms and apps for mental health support. These tools offer virtual counseling, stress-relief techniques, and online mental health assessments. Apps such as **Headspace** and **Mindhouse** are used by many employees for meditation, relaxation, and mental health tracking.

Implementation Insight for HR Professionals: Leverage technology to offer mental health resources through dedicated apps, virtual counseling, and well-being surveys. This will make mental health support more accessible to employees, especially those working remotely or in flexible settings.

7. Mental Health Leave and Policies

Some companies, such as **Tata Steel**, have introduced mental health leave policies that allow employees to take time off to address mental health issues, without the stigma associated with traditional sick leave. These policies help employees recharge and return to work more focused and productive.

Implementation Insight for HR Professionals: Design and implement mental health leave policies that are separate from regular sick leave, ensuring that employees do not have to disclose the nature of their illness. These policies can be supported by awareness programs to educate employees about the importance of taking time off when necessary.

8. Peer Support and Employee Resource Groups (ERGs)

Incorporating Peer Support Groups and ERGs, like those seen in **Accenture** and **Cognizant**, can help create a supportive work environment where employees share experiences and provide mutual support. These groups can focus on mental health awareness, and provide employees with a safe space to discuss issues such as stress, burnout, or anxiety.

Implementation Insight for OB Professionals: Encourage the formation of employee resource groups that focus on mental health and well-being. Allow these groups to collaborate with HR to organize activities that reduce stress and foster community.

9. Feedback Mechanisms and Employee Engagement

Employee engagement surveys and regular feedback mechanisms can be used by HR professionals to gauge the mental health of employees and identify potential issues before they become significant problems. Companies like **Wipro** use pulse surveys to track employee satisfaction and mental health indicators in real-time.

Implementation Insight for HR Professionals: Regularly conduct surveys that include questions specifically related to mental health, stress levels, and overall job satisfaction. Ensure anonymity to encourage honest responses, and use the feedback to improve workplace policies and mental health strategies.

10. Creating Mental Health Ambassadors

Some organizations in India have appointed Mental Health Ambassadors within their teams to champion mental health initiatives and be the first point of contact for employees seeking support. These ambassadors undergo specialized training in mental health first aid and can provide immediate assistance or direct employees to the right resources.

Implementation Insight for HR Professionals: Develop a program that trains select employees as Mental Health Ambassadors, who can act as advocates and provide guidance on mental health issues. These individuals can serve as role models and help reduce stigma in the workplace.

Mental health strategies in Indian companies are evolving rapidly, and HR and OB professionals have a critical role in shaping the mental health landscape within their organizations. By adopting strategies like EAPs, flexible work arrangements, workplace wellness programs, digital tools, and creating supportive cultures, Indian companies are setting a strong foundation for enhancing employee mental health. For management students and professionals, understanding the importance of mental health and integrating these strategies into organizational practices will be crucial for fostering a positive work environment that drives long-term success and employee well-being.

20. HOW STUDENTS CAN APPLY OB PRINCIPLES IN THE WORKPLACE

Organizational Behavior (OB) principles provide valuable frameworks and insights into understanding and managing employee behavior, motivation, teamwork, leadership, and organizational culture. As management students begin to enter the workplace, applying OB principles can enhance their ability to navigate complex organizational dynamics, contribute to effective teamwork, and foster leadership skills. Here's how students can apply OB principles in real-world workplace scenarios:

1. Understanding Motivation and Employee Engagement

One of the foundational principles of OB is understanding what motivates employees. Students can apply **Maslow's Hierarchy of Needs** or **Herzberg's Two-Factor Theory** in their workplaces by recognizing the needs of their colleagues and aligning tasks or goals to fulfill these needs. For instance, if an employee is driven by growth, offering opportunities for professional development or providing challenging work can boost motivation and engagement.

Application in the Workplace: A student can help create an environment where colleagues feel recognized and valued, leading to higher productivity. They can motivate others by understanding intrinsic and extrinsic factors that influence motivation and finding ways to offer both recognition and responsibility based on individual preferences.

2. Effective Communication

OB principles emphasize the importance of clear, open communication in any organization. Miscommunication can lead to misunderstandings, inefficiencies, and conflict. By applying **communication models** (e.g., Shannon-Weaver Model, Transactional Model), students can improve communication processes in the workplace. This includes using active listening, clear messaging, and ensuring feedback is constructive and timely.

Application in the Workplace: Students can actively listen to team members, ask questions to clarify points, and encourage open dialogue in meetings. This will help reduce errors caused by miscommunication and promote a culture of transparency and inclusiveness.

3. Conflict Resolution

Conflict is inevitable in any workplace, but OB theories offer strategies to manage and resolve conflicts constructively. Students can apply **Thomas-Kilmann Conflict Mode Instrument (TKI)**, which outlines five conflict-handling styles: competing, collaborating, compromising, avoiding, and accommodating. By assessing the situation and using the appropriate style, students can help resolve conflicts in a way that benefits both the individuals and the organization.

Application in the Workplace: When conflicts arise, students can apply the principles of collaboration to bring all parties to the table to find mutually agreeable solutions. In instances of workplace disputes, they can act as mediators or guide teams in using a collaborative approach to resolve issues efficiently.

4. Teamwork and Group Dynamics

OB highlights the importance of effective teamwork and the dynamics of groups. Understanding **Tuckman's Stages of Group Development** (forming, storming, norming, performing, adjourning) helps students identify the phase their team is in and take appropriate actions to move the group towards high performance. For example, if a team is in the "storming" phase (characterized by conflict and confusion), students can apply conflict resolution techniques to facilitate better collaboration.

Application in the Workplace: In a project team, students can ensure that team members work cohesively by identifying roles, fostering cooperation, and addressing conflicts quickly to move the team through the necessary stages. They can encourage open communication and offer guidance on the team's goals, helping members understand their contributions to the project's success.

5. Leadership and Influence

Leadership is a crucial component of OB, and students can apply principles such as **transformational leadership**, **situational leadership**, and **servant leadership** to motivate and guide teams. Transformational leaders inspire employees by creating a shared vision and motivating them to go beyond self-interest for the organization's benefit. Situational leadership, on the other hand, teaches students to adapt their leadership style according to the maturity level of the followers and the situation.

Application in the Workplace: Students can apply transformational leadership by setting a strong example and motivating colleagues with a clear vision. By recognizing when to adopt a more directive approach (e.g., for new or inexperienced employees) or a supportive approach (e.g., for highly skilled employees), students can influence and inspire others in a way that maximizes team performance.

6. Organizational Culture and Values

Understanding and navigating an organization's culture is another key OB principle. **Edgar Schein's Organizational Culture Model** helps students identify the underlying assumptions, values, and artifacts that make up an organization's culture. By understanding the company's culture, students can align their behavior with organizational norms and values, which helps build rapport and improve collaboration.

Application in the Workplace: Students should observe and understand their organization's culture and adapt their behavior to fit into it. For example, if an organization values innovation, students can propose creative solutions and suggest new ways of doing things. If the culture values hierarchy, students can respect the chain of command while seeking mentorship and guidance from senior employees.

7. Decision Making

Decision-making is a critical skill in both management and organizational behavior. OB principles highlight various decision-making models, such as the **rational model**, **bounded rationality**, and **intuitive decision-making**. Understanding these models can help students make informed decisions, especially when faced with ambiguity or uncertainty in the workplace.

Application in the Workplace: When faced with a decision, students can follow a systematic approach, such as gathering all relevant information, evaluating options, and considering the impact of their decisions on the organization and its people. By applying OB principles like **groupthink avoidance** and promoting diversity of thought, students can improve the decision-making process and lead to more effective organizational outcomes.

8. Motivating and Recognizing Employees

Effective performance management relies heavily on recognizing and motivating employees. OB theories stress the importance of reinforcement, both positive and negative, in shaping behavior. **Skinner's Operant Conditioning** theory suggests using rewards and recognition to reinforce desired behaviors, such as meeting deadlines or displaying collaboration in team settings.

Application in the Workplace: Students can apply reinforcement techniques by acknowledging good work through praise or rewards, and addressing undesirable behaviors using constructive feedback. This can foster a culture of appreciation and create motivation to consistently perform well.

9. Job Satisfaction and Organizational Commitment

Job satisfaction is one of the central themes in OB, with research suggesting that satisfied employees are more likely to be engaged and committed to the organization. Students can apply **Herzberg's Motivation-Hygiene Theory**, which identifies factors that contribute to job satisfaction (motivators) and dissatisfaction (hygiene factors). By ensuring that employees have adequate resources, recognition, and opportunities for growth, students can help improve job satisfaction within the workplace.

Application in the Workplace: Students can conduct surveys or feedback sessions to gauge employee satisfaction and address issues that may negatively affect motivation. For example, offering opportunities for growth, recognizing achievements, and improving working conditions can contribute to higher employee satisfaction and organizational commitment.

10. Managing Change and Organizational Development

OB provides a foundation for understanding how individuals and organizations respond to change. By applying **Lewin's Change Model** (unfreeze, change, refreeze), students can guide employees through organizational changes. In India, where organizations are increasingly adapting to rapid changes in technology, business processes, and market conditions, students can apply these principles to help manage change effectively and ensure smooth transitions.

Application in the Workplace: When leading or participating in a change initiative, students can use Lewin's model to help employees understand why change is necessary (unfreeze), engage them in the change process (change), and ensure that the changes are embedded into the organization's practices (refreeze). By communicating effectively and addressing concerns, students can ensure that employees feel supported throughout the change process.

Organizational Behavior principles offer management students a comprehensive toolkit for understanding and managing both individual and group behavior in the workplace. By applying these principles—whether through motivating employees, enhancing communication, leading teams, or managing conflict—students can develop the skills necessary to navigate complex workplace environments. As future HR and OB professionals, they will be well-equipped to create organizational cultures that foster collaboration, engagement, and continuous improvement.

---

21. BUILDING A CAREER IN HR: SKILLS AND STRATEGIES

Skills and Strategies in the context of Human Resources (HR) and Organizational Behavior (OB) refer to the essential competencies and approaches that professionals need to effectively manage and lead within organizations. Skills include both technical abilities (such as knowledge of HR processes, recruitment, and performance management) and interpersonal capabilities (like communication, emotional intelligence, and leadership). Strategies are the frameworks or plans organizations use to achieve long-term objectives, such as talent acquisition, employee retention, diversity and inclusion, and organizational development.

Ulrich, D., & Dulebohn, J. H. (2015). *Are We There Yet? What's Next for HR?* Human Resource Management, 54(2), 145-164.

Human Resources (HR) is a dynamic and essential function within any organization. It is responsible for managing employee relations, recruitment, performance management, training and development, and overall organizational culture. For students aspiring to build a career in HR, it's crucial to understand the skills required and the strategies to adopt in order to succeed. The HR profession offers diverse opportunities, from talent acquisition to organizational development, and requires a blend of soft and hard skills, strategic thinking, and continuous learning.

1. Develop Strong Communication Skills

Effective communication is a cornerstone of HR practice. HR professionals need to be adept at both written and verbal communication to interact with employees, resolve conflicts, conduct interviews, and write reports. A significant part of HR work involves conveying policies, explaining benefits, managing negotiations, and fostering a collaborative work environment.

Strategy: Aspiring HR professionals should work on refining their communication skills through practice and seeking feedback. Participating in group discussions, delivering presentations, and writing reports or emails will help in honing these skills. In India, where workplace communication styles may vary due to cultural diversity, it is important to adapt communication methods to the audience.

2. Gain In-depth Knowledge of Labor Laws

In India, labor laws and regulations play a critical role in HR practices. These laws govern various aspects, including employee benefits, workplace safety, discrimination, wage policies, and industrial relations. A solid understanding of these legal frameworks ensures that HR professionals can navigate complex issues and prevent legal challenges.

Strategy: Aspiring HR professionals should pursue certifications in labor laws, such as those offered by professional HR organizations or universities. Staying up-to-date with changes in labor laws is essential to ensure compliance and to advise both employers and employees effectively.

3. Develop Leadership and People Management Skills

HR professionals are often at the forefront of managing people. Whether it's mediating between employees and management, leading training sessions, or guiding team development, leadership skills are essential. People management involves understanding individual motivations, recognizing different personalities, and fostering a positive work environment.

Strategy: To build leadership skills, HR students can participate in leadership development programs, take on leadership roles in student clubs or internships, and practice conflict resolution and team management techniques. These experiences can help develop their ability to lead and inspire others in a professional setting.

4. Master HR Technology and Data Analytics

As HR functions become more data-driven, proficiency with HR software, cloud-based platforms, and HR analytics tools is becoming increasingly important. These tools help HR professionals track performance, manage payroll, and optimize recruitment efforts. In India, where the workforce is diverse, data-driven decisions can significantly improve HR processes.

Strategy: Aspiring HR professionals should gain familiarity with popular HR management systems (HRMS) such as SAP SuccessFactors, Workday, and others. Too, learning basic data analytics skills (Excel, HR analytics tools) can give candidates a competitive edge in HR roles focused on data management, recruitment, and workforce planning.

5. Understand Talent Acquisition and Employee Engagement

Talent acquisition is one of the key responsibilities of HR. HR professionals need to develop strategies for recruiting the right candidates, ensuring diversity, and engaging employees. Understanding how to attract top talent in competitive markets, like India, where demand for skilled labor is high, is crucial.

Strategy: Students can engage in internships or part-time roles within recruitment teams to understand the nuances of talent acquisition. They should also learn the fundamentals of building an employee engagement strategy, focusing on retaining talent, enhancing job satisfaction, and fostering a productive work environment.

6. Be Adaptable to Change and Organizational Development

Organizations are constantly evolving, and HR professionals must be adaptable to changing business needs, technology, and workforce dynamics. HR professionals in India must be especially adaptable as the business environment is rapidly changing with digitalization, shifting labor laws, and globalization.

Strategy: HR students should stay updated on HR trends and global best practices through continuous learning. Engaging with HR communities, attending webinars, and seeking mentorship will help them understand the changing landscape of HR. Too, participating in organizational change management initiatives during internships can provide valuable hands-on experience.

7. Embrace Emotional Intelligence (EQ)

Emotional intelligence is the ability to understand and manage one's emotions as well as the emotions of others. HR professionals often deal with sensitive situations, such as conflict resolution, employee grievances, and performance management. High EQ helps HR professionals handle these challenges with empathy and professionalism, leading to better outcomes.

Strategy: Aspiring HR professionals should focus on building self-awareness, empathy, and social skills through self-reflection, mindfulness practices, and actively listening to others. These skills can be developed through emotional intelligence training programs or by actively engaging with colleagues in various organizational settings.

8. Build Networking and Relationship-Building Skills

HR is a relationship-driven profession. Building a strong network of professional relationships inside and outside the organization is crucial for career success. This includes relationships with employees, leadership teams, external consultants, and vendors. Networking can provide HR professionals with resources, new perspectives, and potential job opportunities.

Strategy: Students can build their professional network by attending HR seminars, webinars, and conferences, joining HR-related social media groups, and seeking mentorship from experienced professionals. Building relationships with peers and faculty during college can also provide valuable long-term connections.

9. Master Strategic Thinking

HR has evolved from an administrative function to a strategic one. HR professionals now play a pivotal role in shaping organizational strategy by aligning human capital with business goals. This requires an understanding of the business, the ability to anticipate future HR needs, and a proactive approach to problem-solving.

Strategy: Aspiring HR professionals should gain an understanding of business fundamentals, financial metrics, and strategic planning. Participating in business-related activities, such as case competitions or company strategy discussions, can help develop the strategic thinking needed in HR. Reading business and leadership books can also enhance their understanding of aligning HR practices with broader organizational goals.

10. Develop Conflict Resolution and Negotiation Skills

Conflict is inevitable in the workplace, and HR professionals are often called upon to mediate and resolve disputes. Being skilled in conflict resolution and negotiation ensures that HR professionals can create solutions that benefit both employees and the organization. In India, where diverse backgrounds and cultural differences are prevalent, handling conflicts with sensitivity is crucial.

Strategy: Students can develop their conflict resolution and negotiation skills through role-playing exercises, attending workshops, and observing HR professionals in action during internships. Understanding the cultural nuances and communication styles within Indian workplaces will further enhance their ability to mediate effectively.

11. Foster Organizational Culture

Organizational culture is central to employee engagement, retention, and performance. HR professionals are responsible for cultivating a positive culture that aligns with the organization's values, mission, and vision. In India, where cultural diversity is prevalent, it's important for HR professionals to create an inclusive and cohesive culture that respects all employees.

Strategy: Students should explore different organizational culture models, such as **Edgar Schein's** framework, and learn how to assess and shape an organization's culture. They should also focus on initiatives that promote diversity and inclusion in the workplace to create an environment where everyone feels valued.

Building a successful career in HR requires a blend of technical knowledge, interpersonal skills, and strategic thinking. Management students who wish to pursue a career in HR must develop a deep understanding of people management, business operations, and organizational behavior. By focusing on essential skills such as communication, leadership, adaptability, legal knowledge, and conflict resolution, HR professionals can help create positive work environments that foster employee engagement, retention, and organizational success. Continuous learning, hands-on experience, and networking will be key to excelling in the ever-evolving field of Human Resources.

22. THE EVOLVING ROLE OF HR AND OB PROFESSIONALS

Human Resources (HR) and Organizational Behavior (OB) professionals have traditionally been responsible for managing employee relations, recruitment, training, and organizational culture. In contempt of that, with the changing landscape of business, advancements in technology, and evolving employee expectations, the role of HR and OB professionals has been rapidly evolving. Today, they are not just administrative support functions but are strategic partners in driving organizational success. This evolution requires HR and OB professionals to be more dynamic, data-driven, and forward-thinking, aligning their roles with the broader goals of the organization.

1. Strategic Partner in Business Growth

Historically, HR was seen primarily as a support function, handling tasks like hiring, payroll, and employee welfare. In contrast, today's HR and OB professionals play a crucial role in shaping the company's strategy. They work closely with leadership to ensure that human capital aligns with the company's long-term vision. This includes identifying the skills needed for the future, shaping organizational culture, and designing employee development programs that match business objectives.

In India, where organizations are facing rapid change due to globalization, technological advancements, and regulatory shifts, HR professionals are increasingly being included in strategic decision-making. For example, HR professionals at large companies like Infosys, Tata Consultancy Services, and Mahindra are now closely involved in business planning, workforce forecasting, and organizational redesign to help companies remain competitive.

2. Employee Experience and Engagement

The importance of employee experience has risen as a central focus in today's work environment. HR and OB professionals are now tasked with shaping an environment that promotes employee engagement, well-being, and job satisfaction. Their role has evolved from managing complaints to fostering a workplace where employees feel connected, valued, and empowered. This is particularly important in India, where employee retention is challenging due to competitive industries and a diverse workforce.

HR professionals are expected to create meaningful experiences through recognition programs, flexible work arrangements, career development opportunities, and initiatives that foster a sense of belonging. OB professionals also contribute by understanding how organizational culture and employee behavior influence the overall work environment. Companies like Zomato, Flipkart, and Mahindra have introduced employee well-being initiatives, such as mental health support, learning programs, and work-life balance policies, which are integral to their HR strategy.

3. Technology and Data Analytics

Technology has revolutionized HR and OB practices. The use of data analytics has allowed HR professionals to make more informed decisions about talent acquisition, employee performance, and retention strategies. In India, where organizations are increasingly adopting technology, HR professionals must leverage tools like Human Resource Management Systems (HRMS), applicant tracking systems, and employee engagement platforms to enhance operational efficiency.

OB professionals are also using data to understand and influence employee behavior and organizational culture. Predictive analytics, for example, can help identify factors that contribute to employee disengagement, enabling organizations to take proactive steps. The rise of Artificial Intelligence (AI) and Machine Learning (ML) in recruitment is also changing the way HR professionals assess candidate fit and predict employee success. By utilizing these technologies, HR and OB professionals can work smarter and ensure that they are optimizing both the employee experience and organizational outcomes.

4. Focus on Diversity, Equity, and Inclusion (DEI)

The importance of diversity, equity, and inclusion (DEI) is gaining traction globally, and Indian organizations are increasingly recognizing the value of a diverse workforce. HR and OB professionals are now responsible for driving DEI initiatives that foster an inclusive work environment, where employees from different backgrounds feel respected and have equal access to opportunities.

In India, where cultural, linguistic, and social diversity is the norm, HR and OB professionals must navigate complex issues related to caste, gender, religion, and regional biases. Leading organizations such as Infosys, Wipro, and Accenture are making DEI a key focus by implementing initiatives that promote gender diversity, ensure equitable pay, and create inclusive policies. HR and OB professionals need to advocate for these changes and develop training programs to educate employees on unconscious biases, inclusivity, and respectful workplace behavior.

5. Change Management and Organizational Development

Organizations today are experiencing constant change, whether it's through mergers and acquisitions, restructuring, or adopting new technologies. HR and OB professionals are key players in managing these changes and ensuring smooth transitions. Their ability to manage change effectively can help minimize resistance, reduce employee anxiety, and ensure alignment with organizational goals.

In India, where companies are increasingly undergoing digital transformation, HR and OB professionals must also address the challenges that come with technological shifts. For example, when large Indian companies like SBI, HDFC, or Maruti Suzuki implement new digital tools or rework their business models, HR professionals are tasked with ensuring that employees are prepared for the change. This includes providing training programs, offering support, and fostering a culture of agility and adaptability within the organization.

6. Workplace Flexibility and Remote Work

The COVID-19 pandemic accelerated the shift toward remote and hybrid work models. As a result, HR and OB professionals now play a critical role in managing this transition and ensuring that remote work policies are effective. This includes addressing challenges such as employee isolation, maintaining productivity, and fostering collaboration in virtual environments.

In India, where remote work was initially met with skepticism, companies like TCS and Wipro have successfully implemented flexible work arrangements that balance employee needs with business objectives. HR professionals are responsible for developing policies that ensure employees remain engaged, connected, and productive while working remotely. Over and above, they must ensure that all employees, whether working remotely or on-site, feel equally valued and included in company activities and decision-making.

7. Learning and Development

The rapidly changing business environment demands continuous learning and skill development. HR professionals are responsible for designing and implementing learning programs that enable employees to acquire new skills, particularly in areas like digital transformation, leadership, and emotional intelligence. OB professionals contribute by understanding how motivation, job satisfaction, and organizational culture influence learning outcomes.

In India, where rapid economic development has led to new industries and job roles, HR and OB professionals must be proactive in identifying skills gaps and fostering a culture of continuous learning. Companies like Reliance Industries and Infosys have invested heavily in training programs and leadership development initiatives to ensure that employees have the skills to thrive in the evolving business landscape.

The role of HR and OB professionals is evolving from a traditional administrative function to a strategic one that directly influences business success. As the business environment becomes more complex, HR and OB professionals must adapt to new challenges, including technological advancements, the changing nature of work, and the growing focus on diversity and employee well-being. In India, where businesses are experiencing rapid growth and transformation, the ability to navigate these changes effectively is crucial for HR and OB professionals. By embracing strategic thinking, data-driven decision-making, and a focus on employee engagement and development, HR and OB professionals can drive sustainable organizational success in the future.

AUTHOR PROFILE

Dr. Dhanashree Chaudhari is an Assistant Professor in the Department of Management Studies at KCES's Institute of Management and Research, Jalgaon. She holds an MBA (HR), DLL & LW, M. Com, and a Ph.D., specializing in Perceived Organizational Support and Employee Engagement.

With over nine years of experience in teaching and research, Dr. Chaudhari has published seven research papers and presented eight conference papers. Her expertise spans Human Resource Development, Employee Engagement, Organizational Behavior, and General Management.

Passionate about enhancing workplace dynamics, Dr. Chaudhari's research focuses on Organizational Behavior and the evolving landscape of modern Human Resource Management.

Dr. Dipali Patil is an Assistant Professor in the Department of Management Studies at KCES's Institute of Management and Research, Jalgaon. She holds an MBM (PM), MBA (HR), M.Com, and a Ph.D., with a specialization in work stress and coping approaches.

With over nine years of experience in teaching and research, Dr. Patil has published 12 research papers and presented 14 conference papers. Her areas of expertise include Human Resource Development, Stress Management, Business Research Methods, Digital Transformation, and Work-Life Integration.

Driven by a passion for enhancing workplace environments, Dr. Patil's research focuses on integrating modern Human Resource practices with Organizational Behavior to foster innovation and well-being in professional settings.

REFERENCES

1. Defining HR and OB in Modern Workplaces
Smith, J. (2020). *Human resources and organizational behavior: A guide to modern workplace dynamics.* Business Insights Press.

2. Hollenbeck, J. R., & Wright, P. M. (2021). Organizational behavior and its evolution in contemporary settings. *Journal of Organizational Behavior,* 42(3), 189-205.

3. Importance of People-Centric Management
Patel, R. (2021). Building a people-first workplace: A case study approach. *Human Resource Management Journal,* 34(4), 72-81.

4. Gallo, C. (2020). *The power of people: How people-centric management drives business results.* Harvard Business Press.

5. Virtual and Hybrid Organizations
Guo, Y., & Zhang, W. (2021). The rise of hybrid organizations in the post-pandemic era. *Journal of Business and Technology,* 25(2), 115-130.

6. Turner, P. (2020). *Workplace transformation: Embracing hybrid and virtual teams.* Oxford Business Publishing.

7. Recruitment Strategies for Millennials and Gen Z
McDonald, J. K. (2020). Adapting recruitment strategies

for the new workforce. *Journal of Human Resource Development*, 58(1), 45-60.

8. Sharma, P., & Desai, R. (2021). Reaching Millennials and Gen Z: Modern recruitment strategies. *Indian Journal of HRM*, 29(2), 72-89.

9. AI in Hiring: Tools and Techniques
   Kumar, A., & Yadav, S. (2021). Leveraging artificial intelligence in recruitment. *Journal of Digital HR*, 17(4), 22-36.

10. Rana, T. (2022). *AI in HR: The future of hiring and recruitment*. Springer Publishing.

11. Role of AI, ML, and Blockchain in HR
    Patel, K., & Singh, R. (2021). Machine learning in HR: Transforming human resources operations. *International Journal of HR Technology*, 8(3), 35-50.

12. Sharma, V., & Gupta, N. (2020). *Blockchain for HR: How emerging technologies are shaping the future of HR management*. BusinessTech Press.

13. Automation and Its Impact on HR and OB
    Brown, A., & Miller, D. (2021). The future of work: Automation's role in HR and organizational behavior. *Journal of Labor Studies*, 16(2), 94-107.

14. Kapoor, S. (2020). *Automation in HR: Embracing change and technology*. Harvard Business Review.

15. The Role of OKRs and KPIs
    Kumar, S., & Sharma, N. (2021). Implementing OKRs and KPIs for enhanced performance in modern organizations. *Business Performance Review*, 31(1), 28-42.

16. Williams, R., & Harris, C. (2022). *OKRs and KPIs: The framework for success in the modern workplace*. McGraw Hill.

17. Upskilling and Reskilling the Workforce
Rathi, S. (2020). Upskilling the workforce: Meeting the challenges of tomorrow's jobs. *Journal of Workforce Development*, 44(1), 12-25.

18. Hameed, T. (2021). *The future of work: Upskilling and reskilling strategies in HR*. Business Insights Journal, 20(2), 41-58.

19. Equity and Transparency in Pay Structures
Patel, D., & Shah, M. (2021). Pay transparency and its impact on organizational culture. *Indian Journal of Organizational Behavior*, 33(1), 99-112.

20. Gupta, P., & Yadav, T. (2020). *Pay equity and fairness: The future of compensation management*. HR Innovations Press.

21. Strategies for Reducing Attrition
Nair, L., & Verma, S. (2020). Reducing employee attrition: Effective retention strategies in HR. *Journal of HR Research*, 28(4), 76-89.

22. Sharma, P. (2021). *Employee retention strategies: Reducing attrition in modern workplaces*. Sage Publishing.

23. Emotional Intelligence and Self-Awareness
Singh, S., & Thakur, R. (2020). Emotional intelligence in leadership: Implications for HR. *Indian Journal of Organizational Psychology*, 40(2), 122-134.

24. Goleman, D. (2019). *Emotional intelligence: Why it can matter more than IQ*. Bantam Books.

25. Building High-Performing Teams
Kumar, A., & Mishra, P. (2021). Building high-performing teams: A practical guide for HR leaders. *Journal of Organizational Development*, 23(3), 49-60.

26. Smith, J. (2020). *Team dynamics and performance: How to build and sustain high-performing teams.* McKinsey & Company Publishing.

27. Building Inclusive Cultures
Sharma, N. (2020). Diversity and inclusion: Creating inclusive organizational cultures. *Journal of Diversity Management,* 37(1), 41-53.

28. Shaw, A. (2021). *Building inclusive cultures in the workplace: An actionable guide.* Penguin Business Press.

29. Measuring DEI Success
Patel, R. (2021). Measuring the success of diversity, equity, and inclusion initiatives. *Journal of Organizational Studies,* 29(4), 105-118.

30. Jain, S., & Gupta, N. (2020). *Effective DEI metrics: How to measure success and impact.* Springer Publishing.

31. Sustainability Practices and Employee Advocacy
Agarwal, S. (2021). Sustainability in the workplace: Integrating environmental and social practices. *Journal of Corporate Responsibility,* 32(2), 51-64.

32. Chopra, A. (2020). *Sustainability and employee advocacy: A guide for modern businesses.* Tata McGraw-Hill.

33. The Gig Economy and Remote Work
Desai, M., & Kumar, R. (2021). The gig economy and the future of work: An Indian perspective. *Journal of Indian Business Studies,* 43(5), 155-169.

34. Mehta, R. (2020). *The gig economy in India: A roadmap to flexible work.* Indian Business Publishing.

35. The Change Curve and Employee Adaptability
Kumar, S. (2020). Adapting to organizational change: Understanding the change curve. *Journal of Business Management,* 25(1), 88-102.

Bridges, W. (2019). *Managing transitions: Making the most of change.* Harvard Business Review Press.

36. Mental Health Initiatives in Modern Workplaces Verma, S. (2021). Mental health at work: Effective initiatives for the modern workplace. *Journal of Occupational Health,* 12(2), 34-45.

37. Chopra, K. (2020). *Mental health in organizations: Strategies for creating supportive work environments.* Springer Publishing.

38. How Students Can Apply OB Principles in the Workplace Sharma, R., & Singh, P. (2021). Applying organizational behavior principles in the workplace: A student's guide. *Management Journal of India,* 18(4), 45-59.

39. Robbins, S. P. (2019). *Organizational Behavior.* Pearson Education India.

40. Building a Career in HR: Skills and Strategies Khanna, R. (2021). Building a career in HR: Essential skills and strategies for success. *Human Resource Development Review,* 29(3), 112-123.

41. Taylor, P., & Green, S. (2020). *The HR career path: Strategies for success.* Sage Publications.

42. The Evolving Role of HR and OB Professionals Shah, K. (2021). The evolving role of HR and OB professionals in India. *Indian Journal of HRM,* 41(3), 109-120.

43. Mello, J. A. (2020). *Strategic human resource management.* Cengage Learning.

44. Ulrich, D., & Dulebohn, J. H. (2015). *Are We There Yet? What's Next for HR?* Human Resource Management, 54(2), 145-164.

45. World Health Organization (WHO). (2004). *Promoting Mental Health: Concepts, Emerging Evidence, Practice.* WHO

46. Kubler-Ross, E. (1969). *On Death and Dying.* Macmillan.

47. Kalleberg, A. L., & Dunn, M. (2016). Good Jobs, Bad Jobs in the Gig Economy. Economic Policy Institute.

48. Boudreau, K. J., & Lakhani, K. R. (2013). Using the Crowd as an Innovation Input: A Case Study of the Pet-Co-Creation Project. Harvard Business School.

49. Venkatesh, P. (2018). Gig Economy in India: Opportunities and Challenges. Journal of Business Research, 9(1), 29-38.

50. Hart, S. L. (1995). A Natural-Resource-Based View of the Firm. Academy of Management Review, 20(4), 986-1014.

51. Elkington, J. (1998). Cannibals with Forks: The Triple Bottom Line of 21st Century Business. Capstone.

52. Schaltegger, S., & Wagner, M. (2017). Managing the Transition to a Sustainable Enterprise: Corporate Social Responsibility and Sustainability in Business Practice. Springer.

53. Agarwal, R. (2018). Corporate Sustainability Practices in India: An Overview. International Journal of Business and Management Studies, 8(1), 12-25.

54. Cox, T. (1994). Cultural Diversity in Organizations: Theory, Research & Practice. Berrett-Koehler.

55. Shore, L. M., Cleveland, J. N., & Sanchez, D. (2011). Inclusive workplaces: A review and model. Human Resource Management Review, 21(1), 3-10.

56. Mor Barak, M. E. (2015). Inclusion is the key to diversity management: Re-conceptualizing diversity for organizational effectiveness. Sage Publications.

57. Shore, L. M., Cleveland, J. N., & Sanchez, D. (2011). Inclusive workplaces: A review and model. Human Resource Management Review, 21(1), 3-10.

58. Katzenbach, J. R., & Smith, D. K. (1993). The Wisdom of Teams: Creating the High-Performance Organization. HarperBusiness.

59. Goleman, D. (1995). Emotional Intelligence: Why It Can Matter More Than IQ. Bantam Books.

60. Price, J. L. (1977). The Study of Turnover. Iowa State University Press.

61. Bersin, J. (2018). The Employee Experience: How to Attract Talent, Develop Talent, and Keep Talent. Deloitte Review, 22.

62. Doerr, J. (2018). Measure What Matters: OKRs: The Simple Idea that Drives 10x Growth. Portfolio Penguin.

63. Harrison, J., & Shipman, J. (2019). The Rise of HR Technology: Automation and its Impact on the Workforce. Human Resource Management Review, 29(2), 197-209.

All the Best!